THE POWER OF
ACTING

Hi Tim,

Love
Josephine

First edition 2016

ISBN: 978-0-9955455-0-2

Design and graphics: Louise Burston

Printed in South Wales

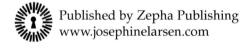 Published by Zepha Publishing
www.josephinelarsen.com

THE POWER OF
ACTING

discovering the person
behind the mask

JOSEPHINE LARSEN

For
Michelle and Max

Go into the arts. I'm not kidding. The arts are not a way to make a living. They are a very human way of making life more bearable. Practicing an art, no matter how well or badly, is a way of making your soul grow, for heaven's sake. Dance to the radio. Tell stories. Write a poem to a friend, even a lousy poem. Do it as well as you possibly can. You will get an enormous reward. You will have created something.
Kurt Vonnegut

ACKNOWLEDGEMENTS

A THOUSAND THANKS to all the creative players and artists I have had the honour of sharing time, space and energy with, every single one of you. You have shown me that everyone is unique, that imagination never dies and that there can be only one absolute truth and that is LOVE.

Thanks also to all the teachers, directors, colleagues and friends who have in some way shaped who I am now. Above all:

Joyce Corfield –'Corky', an old Pro' Drama Teacher at Farlington School for Girls, Sussex, who, when I was 11 years old somehow mysteriously managed to get permission for me to miss a lot of main lessons like geography, history and maths in order to rehearse school plays. She showed me that I could be anything I wanted to be, including a mad woman with a seagull on my hat, a man, a fool and a tree. She was one in a million and she saved my life.

Nat Brenner – principal of Bristol Old Vic Theatre School (B.O.V.T.S), who taught me that there is beauty in all things and that one of the most important acting skills is to listen.

Rudi Shelley – Russian Jewish survivor of the concentration camps, master of ballet and acting tutor at B.O.V.T.S., who taught me how to stand tall and said: 'If it is not easy, darling, you're not doing it right.'

Budd Thompson – American dancer, teacher and choreographer in Copenhagen, who introduced me to dancing naked with no shame amidst a troupe of utterly gorgeous gay guys.

Daniel Sanders – choreographer of Les Folles de Paris, who witnessed me polishing off 24 oysters and a bottle of Chardonnay *before* I danced the lead role in a show in Paris, and then invited me to come to Berlin and turned me into a 'star' of the Berlin Cabaret scene.

Ian McNaughton – Director, producer and writer for the Monty Python's Flying Circus, who directed me in a late-night German T.V. comedy show and taught me that the most important ingredient of play is 'joy'.

Rik Maverik – a black, gay, New York ghetto 'sister' with knife slashes on his chest and debt collectors on his back, director of the Berlin Play Actors, who taught me to not worry about money and 'just do it'.

Maximillian Glass – Hermaphrodite, classical pianist, natural crystal expert, who confirmed my beliefs about the relationship between space and time and introduced me to many other wonders of the Universe.

Peter Oswald – Poet, playwright, actor, once resident writer at the Globe, London, also writer for the National Theatre, London, and his beautiful wife Alice Oswald (T.S.Eliot Award), with whom I spent ten important creative years, who taught me much about the music and magic of words and the spaces in between them.

I'd also like to thank some of the other genius thinkers I have encountered, albeit in books or on the internet, some dead, some living today, some personal aquaintences ... Lao Tsu, William Shakespeare, William Blake, William Wordsworth, Samuel Taylor Coleridge, Charles Fourier, Lautreamont, Paul Lafargue, George Gurdjieff, Antonin Artaud, Abraham Maslow, Franz Mesmer, Jerzy Grotowski, Carl Jung, Alan Watts, Rudolf Steiner, Joseph Campbell, Fritz Perls, Augustus Boal, Carlos Castaneda, James Hillman, William Burroughs, Richard Bandler, Erich Neuman, Robert Crookall, Stanislav Grof, Terence McKenna, Rupert Sheldrake, Neil Gaiman, Hunter S. Thompson, Eckhart Tolle, Stella Adler, Keith Johnstone, Alice Walker, Angela Carter, Bjork, Russel Brand, Lynne McTaggart, Llys Dana, Will Self and Gerry King ... there are doubtless countless others, but they don't spring to the front of my mind right now. I'm sure there have to be more women ... Andrea Dworkin, Marianne Segebrecht, Eleanora Carrington, Queen Elizabeth I, Emmeline Pankhurst and all the other outstanding rebels who have managed to change the course of history in some way.

Finally, a very special thanks to Jeremy Holloway, Bardot Boy, Anna Ash, Jessica Hatchett, David Ash, Michael Pickles, Barbara Homzuik, Michael Brown, Claire Patrick, Jaques Juin, Priscilla Bergey and of course in particular, Louise Burston (and her daughter Eleni) for so generously giving me their time to read what I have written, comment on, edit, shape and create this book. All of them have given me great encouragement, inspiration, vital tips and advice (albeit all from completely different perspectives) without which this book would not have been possible.

INTRODUCTION

THERE ARE MANY books out there about how to succeed as a professional stage or film actor. I recommend some of my favourites at the end of this book. So why write another? Because an actor's training is clearly not just about 'stage worthiness'. Nor is it just about being believable on film or in front of a camera. Acting is a LIFE SKILL. It is a highly intelligent form of imaginative play that teaches us about ourselves and others. It touches on every aspect of being human, emotionally, sensually, mentally, physically and mystically, and it does this in the most experientially inter-active and amusing way possible. Perhaps most important of all, learning to act requires the development of evolved communication skills, human understanding and empathy, which are desperately needed in the world today.

Taught in the right way, acting can greatly increase ones self-belief, confidence and motivation for life in very simple and effective ways. For example, *slow down, take your time, breathe, watch, listen, feel, do nothing, imagine, trust your intuition, be truthful, only do something if you really feel it*. Were you ever taught these things at school? These are some of the most empowering and effective techniques that professional actors use to immerse themselves in the action or the role they are playing.

I believe learning to act is as important a subject as reading, writing and maths.

Not everyone wants to become an actor. Not everyone wants to become a mathematician or engineer either. What works for one may be completely wrong for another. Behind the facade of whoever we are or pretend to be, I trust that we know which 'way' works best for us.

Nevertheless, for a long time now, I have noticed that people in general tend to be fascinated by the skills of accomplished actors. This is perhaps understandable, considering the amount of money and glamorous attention that top actors get! But, I think there is much more to it than this. Skilled actors appear to have some mercurial, transformative skills that other people don't have, some kind of charisma or playful power that many 'ordinary' people would love to make their own.

For me it is clear. One cannot separate the art of acting from any other human activity, whether it be nursing, teaching, policing, science, astrology, history, geography, maths, sport, sewing or gardening, because imagination is central to all human creation and our evolution.

> Imagination is more important than knowledge.
> Knowledge is limited. Imagination encircles the world.
>
> Albert Einstein

On the basis of this, I am compelled to write about the Playground that I have been nurturing and the extraordinary human transformations that I have witnessed when teaching professional acting techniques to people who wouldn't normally describe themselves as 'actors'. Over the years, I have gathered some radical insights into the true nature of the human spirit and developed a large range of alternative resources, which I wish to share.

In the first chapter, I describe the nature of the Playground and who can play. (Please note that in Shakespearian times actors were called *players*.)

The second chapter tells the story of my own personal relationship with professional acting and the evolution of the Playground. It includes my observations of clear correlations between the 'art of acting' and modern paradigms in psychology, neurology and life skills.

The third chapter is a provocative enquiry into why we are not taught these things in school and, considering its general relevance in all walks of life, why the vast majority of young adults enter the job world knowing absolutely nothing about acting or about their true potential as imaginative beings in life.

The fourth chapter discloses some of the acting secrets that I explore and explains the Playground's conceptual principles and processes.

The fifth gives detailed descriptions of a large range of the games, techniques and creative challenges that I have invented or developed for use in the Playground ... the sixth briefly discusses: 'What now?'

In essence, this is an account of my own personal discovery process as a professional actress and a rather rebellious player on this planet. It's an exploration of the invisible spaces between the things that we are led to believe are true.

Looking back, I can see how my rebellious curiosity, my resistance to mainstream arts entertainment and the competitiveness of the profession,was nothing more or less than a search for some other kind of truth, integrity and authenticity in the 'real world'; the outcomes of which I was predestined to share with others.

Sometimes I state the obvious, because the screamingly obvious needs to be stated. Sometimes I refer to acting concepts and techniques that are not so obvious, but which are profoundly relevant to the untapped potential of the human mind and spirit.

I do not claim that anything I suggest or write about is new or even completely mine. I therefore include referenced quotes from many of the great minds who have influenced what I think and feel today, in order to inspire the reader to question and research further.

This book represents a piecing together of observations, strangely synchronistic events, quotes, ideas, theoretical musings and case studies, plus a large collection of absurd games and imaginative challenges that embrace a whole range of what may initially appear to be disparate subjects. My intention is to lead the reader, as I do the players in the Playground, via a series of fascinating insights towards a greater awareness of the role of the Creative Observer and the relationship between his/her inner Shadow world of imagination and the world we live in.

I have two small notes to add.

One is about my use of gender pronouns. The pronoun 'it' implies that one is an object, so, except in the case of a case study, where I have respected the choice of the individual with regard to the gender or the role they wish to play in society, I have chosen to use *s/he* or an elongated pronoun, *him/her* or *his/hers*. In this way, I wish to address the taboo that denies one the right to say that one is something in between the two, or in part, both at once.

One other small point. It is often said that teachers of the performing arts are failed actors. This type of generalisation is outdated and naively misleading, when considering the greater potential of the art of acting. For me, both acting and teaching acting was a means of discovering this potential. It is my hope that this book will provide some vital and playful suggestions not just for aspiring actors and teachers of the performing arts, but for teachers in general, wherever or in whatever subject or field they are active. It is my aim to show that the development of acting and improvisation skills can help literally anyone to become a more creative, confident, responsive, intuitive, self-aware, inter-connected, in touch, focused, empowered, empathic, free, daring, heroic, proactive, imaginative, communicative, compassionate, joyous, unique and playful individual in the theatre of life.

Josephine Larsen 2016

Players' Testimonies

'Josephine, Thank you for the acting group tonight ... you must get told this a lot but I must say it too ... This is something amazing that you're doing.'

'You are the best teacher in the world; with a very special and unique talent for teasing out of us, our hidden selves. You hold an exceptional physical and emotional beauty, grace and enigma. You're one in a trillion. So glad I came back to your classes!'

'[I've gained] ... a sense of belonging. A deep respect for the bravery of others, a lessening of my own self-importance and a lessening of the fear of failure.'

'It is absolutely incredible!! The funkiest way to begin the week and the most amazing journey ... I truly thank you for doing what you do so well.'

CONTENTS

Acknowledgements   v

Introduction   vii

Chapter One: Oases for Child-like Play   1

Chapter Two: Parallel Worlds   15

Chapter Three: Invisible Walls   33

Chapter Four: The Mirror   45

Chapter Five: The Games   95

    Part One: The Approach   98

    Part Two: The Imagination   110

    Part Three: Transformation and Truth   131

    Part Four: The Underbelly   157

Afterword: What Next?   173

About the Author   177

Every child is an artist. The problem is how to remain an artist once we grow up.   Pablo Picasso

CHAPTER ONE

OASES FOR
CHILD-LIKE PLAY

AN ADULT PLAYGROUND

I WAS CURIOUS to know why people kept telling me that what I offered didn't exist anywhere else. So, I searched the World Wide Web. I typed the name THE ADULT PLAYGROUND (which is what I called it at the time) into the search engines and ... found a plethora of pornographic sites. I wasn't surprised. My choice of name was intentional – a provocative jab precisely at the fact that 'the adult playground' is generally understood to refer to pornography; probably the biggest and most profitable industry in the world, alongside chemistry and war fare. These are not the games I play.

Other than that, I found one solitary company in America that provides Adult Playgrounds for obese people; activity parks, they call them, with swings and roundabouts and bouncy castles, designed to attract adults who don't normally take much physical exercise. It is not my intention to provide fun weight-loss programmes either.

I changed the name. I now call it simply the *Playground* and that is how I refer to it throughout the book.

I continued my search.

In an artistic context, I found adult play groups all over Europe and America that explore *imagination, improvisation* and *self-expression* in more or less exclusive or overlapping cross-art-forms: experimental dance, contact improvisation, clowning, fool work, comedy stand-up, forum theatre, playback theatre, improvised street theatre, arts therapy and psychodrama. I include elements of all of these forms of play in the Playground, so why were people telling me that nothing like this exists elsewhere?

A very subtle, but major difference began to emerge. I found no other such like Playground that explores *professional* acting techniques with the primary aim of empowering individuals (both actors and non-actors) with essential LIFE and COMMUNICATION SKILLS.

Top stage and film acting techniques are usually taught in the context of making people 'stage or film worthy'. Furthermore these techniques are usually only taught to a relative small minority i.e. those who are considered talented enough to gain entry into top drama schools. Funnily enough, the ones that are selected are usually those who demonstrate in some way that they already know how to do it. Knowledge of this enlightening kind is guarded by 'the professionals', like magicians guard their tricks of illusion.

I began asking myself two things: 'Why shouldn't the common player be empowered by these top secrets, when the results are so clearly transformational?' and 'Why is there such a strong divide between theatre and life itself?'

The most obvious answer to the latter question is that life is 'real' and theatre isn't. Theatre and film are simulations of life. We dream of doing things on stage and in film that we wouldn't dream of doing in real life. Of course! But in my rather anarchic mind this observation inspires far deeper questions about the very real connection between life and imaginative play. I mean, how on earth do we create the world we live in? The whole of life could be seen as a form of theatre or film.

One question led to another and in my on-going research I came across like minds ... a whole zeitgeist phenomenon, if you like, that must have begun at least two centuries ago ... alternative thinkers, writers, spiritual teachers, psychologists, philosophers, actors, and theatre directors and yes, quantum physicists and scientists too, who express opinions similar to mine. We are creative observers.

> **In the Copenhagen interpretation of quantum reality, things are considered to exist only to the extent that they are observed. Consciousness is the observer.**
>
> David Ash, *Vortex of Energy*, 2012:127

In short, we are in need of nothing short of a revolution in our common consciousness; a new general awareness of the potential of the human psyche, imagination, intuitive intelligence and the real nature of the human mind. We need an awakened perception of a universe, in which the word 'separate' no longer exists.

Sadly, we witness the opposite. The 'success' of industrial and capitalist (profit orientated) progress has turned us into full time blinkered, right brained, for the most part robotic and sedentary workaholics, living in our separate little microcosms. Stressed out of our minds, isolated from each other (apart from on Facebook), with no time to truly sense or dream, we have to accept that we have been dumbed down to become willing and unwilling consumers, money addicted slaves, albeit with a longer life expectancy, but exhausted, dis-eased beings, who in their play time sit hypnotically captivated by billion dollar films starring our favourite actors...whom we attempt to emulate or copy.

> **A strange delusion possesses the working classes of the nations where capitalist civilization holds its sway. This delusion drags in its train the individual and social woes which for two centuries have tortured sad humanity. This delusion is the love of work ...**
>
> Paul Lafargue, 1883 *The Right to be Lazy*, written in Saint Saint Pélagie Prison

It is time to exit an era, in which we have been told that the only route to success or freedom is speed and slavery.

Gradually it dawned on me why something as simple as the concept of enabling people to slow down, imagine and dream; to gain access to their intuitive/emotional intelligence; to empathise with others; to self-actualise through dramatic games and spontaneous play might well, in this day and age, be regarded as unusual, alternative, airy-fairy, gay, weird and probably dangerous.

> **I have a theory that the truth is never told during the nine-to-five hours.**
>
> Hunter. S. Thompson, maverick American Journalist.
> *Fear and Loathing in Las Vegas*

Very recently, I saw a video clip of John Cleese (*Monty Python's Flying Circus*) giving a lecture to a large Flemish audience, all very corporate in appearance, at a World Creativity Forum. He was lecturing on the theme of *'Creating Oases for Childlike Play'*.

Cleese said that if you're racing around all day, ticking things off a list, looking at your watch, making phone calls and generally just keeping all the balls in the air, you are not going to have any creative ideas, which is why the offices of companies like Google are full of toys, why the workdays of the *Mad Men* 'creatives' often resemble preschool and why artists' work spaces tend to be so intriguing to peer into. They are, as Cleese terms them, 'oases' from the punishing pace of the workaday world. He was suggesting that the unconscious mind is a genius source of creative intelligence that comes into play when we are asleep and when the logical mind is switched off.

But it was the following part of his lecture that kept returning to haunt me:

> **... if people in charge are very egotistical, then they want to take credit for everything that happens and they want to feel that they are in control of everything that happens and that means that, consciously or unconsciously, they will discourage creativity in other people.**
>
> John Cleese, www.openculture.com

Powerful, confident, relaxed and visionary creative play i.e. doing what we feel like doing, using our intuitive intelligence, imagining and dreaming, appears to be the privilege of the ones in control; the high ranking 'smart' kids, royalty, the rich, the famous, the well-connected, the super talented and the lucky. One could contest that not even they know much about it, because they are so restricted by their good fortunes. Either way, creative play, I mean the type of imaginative, experiential play that I am describing in this book, appears not to be for your 'average punter'.

I would like to point out very quickly that when I use phrases like 'common player', 'average punter', 'normal' human beings or the word 'reality', I am merely being facetious. I do not believe that anyone is normal or average, and I believe that we all need to ask far more questions about what is prescribed to us as being 'normality' or 'reality'.

> **Imagine a world...rescued from psychopaths by a children's game invented by adult prodigies...in fact, stop imagining – and become more than we have dreamed or dared.**
>
> Darin Stevenson, visionary writer.
> Posted on Facebook 2015

What sort of children's games are we talking about? *Hide and Seek*? *Here We Go Round the Mulberry Bush*? *Simon Says*? *Wink Murder*? *Let's Pretend*? *Charades*? Yes. And the '*Ministry of Silly Walks Tag*' too. And '*Secret Missions*' and '*Absurd Habits*' and '*Power Swops*' and '*That's Not How The Story Goes*' ... and much more.

What's missing are oases in time and space, where adults can re-unite with the child in themselves again, where no-one is competing to be the best, where there aren't any fixed rules (except that we don't hurt each other intentionally) and where failure is not a concept. I am not saying: 'Failure is not an option'. I am saying that the word 'failure' doesn't exist. We need playgrounds where we can re-invent ourselves, re-define the word 'success' and *unlearn* some of the life-debilitating and soul-destroying rules that we learnt in school.

If you're interested read on, but be warned, this book is biased in favour of a healthy curiosity for the forbidden and the absurdly unacceptable. I am talking about a new, but very ancient game, which involves *a lot of imagination* and which has the power to transform our lives and take us into other 'psychic realities'. We all know how to play this game. Some better than others ... we call them ACTORS.

> **In fact he* [the actor] may be said to be the most experienced and adept performer of the whole gamut of social skills and activities. If he is this, and I believe the accomplished actor has this potential, then we must take the actor very seriously indeed. He is capable**

of bringing back from his explorations a mass of sociological information, and does this experientially, not from the detached, impersonal and limited view point of an outside observer.

Clive Barker, Professional Actor, Director and Teacher,
Theatre Games 1977:213

* an example of how gender specific pronouns can appear to be discriminatory.

The Playground sessions that I facilitate exist somewhere between theatre and reality, in a virtual zone that is more real than reality. They find their setting in unpretentious places, where one might least expect to find them, in an office, a community room, on the street, in a ruin, the back-room of a pub or someone's living room (if there is enough room to run around a bit), nothing fancy. I create spaces where people can turn off their smart phones and pick up where they left off years ago, when they were told as children to stop mucking about. I cultivate oases, safe zones, where people can rediscover what imagination is really about; where they can create a universe out of nothing.

In these spaces, I have watched adults of all ages and genders transform into the opposite of what they pretend to be in everyday life. There are no rules, no boundaries, but paradoxically, this is where the individual learns, possibly for the first time *consciously* in their life, to define and create his/her *own* boundaries. They learn how to say YES and NO whenever and to whatever they want to.

In the professional acting dimension, the first skill and act of empowerment is to know what you really *feel* and *want*. What is your intention? What is the nature of your *relationship* with the world around you? The problem for non-actors being: How can we know these things, when we are constantly told throughout life not to do things we want to do and to do things we don't want to do? Who am 'I' in 'reality?

In essence, this is what professional actors do. We study *roles* and *parts* and *plays*. We explore the relationship between the roles and parts we play and the energetic fields around us. We learn to manage space and time and energy. We learn to become confident and emotionally intelligent. Accomplished actors learn to be spontaneous, flexible and attentive in the moment. In the NOW. We learn about the *power of imagination*, and the effect of it. We learn about *truth*, one's own and others', about *presence, listening, direct eye-contact, authenticity* and *speaking from the heart*. Contrary to what most people believe, we learn *not* to pretend. Acting is not about pretending.

All these 'tricks' are in fact vital LIFE SKILLS, which, even if visited briefly, have the potential of radically shifting one's understanding of the world and the imagined roles one plays in it.

Some players shy away from such revelatory freedom. Understandably. Our fears and our shadows come to light like powerful jokers in this *acting dimension*. It is so potent that some back off, fearing exposure in the spotlight perhaps. There are aspects of the play which touch on and awaken the inner core of one's being. The majority though, welcome this as a truly life giving breath of fresh air and a delicious escape from the stressful and often utterly boring oppression of 'normality'.

The Playgrounds that I nurture are much needed oases, where adults can recover and re-discover parts of themselves that were denied them as children at play; curious, creative, demanding, intuitive and astutely intelligent parts that were dumbed down or suppressed in a striving for acceptance in what we call the 'real' world.

Dangers and risks? Yes, of course. But no more than in 'real life'. In some ways the risks are less, because things that one would not normally dare do or say in the 'real world' can be tried out and tested, applauded even, in this rather theatrical, but safe play zone, elevated out of 'normality' into another reality, more authentic than the real world.

I'm the happiest when I'm actually doing this sort of stuff. It's weird. It's more real than the real thing or life, if that makes sense!

Player's testimony

In other ways the risks are more, because there are no guarantees that things will work out the way they are intended. This may initially be terrifying for some. But this is the brilliance of this sort of heightened creative play. It's unpredictable! It's how one can best learn to think creatively on one's feet and become ingeniously flexible, spontaneous, courageous and, yes, truly powerful. This is where the edge lies. This is where the revolution begins.

Is This Therapy?

In the acting profession we have this phenomenon called 'Doctor Theatre'. I personally have experienced it many times. What was a severe back problem or a pain *before* a performance, more often than not disappears completely when *in character on stage*. It can disappear altogether or is significantly reduced even *after* the performance. In the Playground I have witnessed similar transformations. Time and time again, I have watched how a player, who appears old and restricted in 'real life', can come across as miraculously young and agile during the games, as if some kind of weight had magically fallen away from their being. I have also witnessed how these temporary transformations, given time, can become conscious and permanent personality changes in the players' everyday lives, like roles or hidden parts that grow up or come out and play.

And yet, acting is often considered to be a 'pretentious' art form; a vain and exhibitionist pursuit of attention seeking.

Some people, including many professional psychoanalysts, believe that performers are social misfits – immature, exhibitionist people who have never grown up properly, or neurotics engaged in a programme of self-treatment.

Glenn D Wilson, Psychologist,
Psychology for Performing Artists, 1994:167

In many ways this is true. The acting and entertainment profession invites massive egos that are constantly striving to be acknowledged and appreciated! But one can probably find similar child-like egos, desperately trying to reinvent themselves in order to be accepted, in any walk of life. Even in the Houses of Parliament. We vote these people into power. Maybe we are all immature misfits, who have never grown up properly, in a world where we are led to believe that the 'fittest' survive, but where the 'fittest' seem to be hell bent on global destruction. Maybe we need to redefine what 'fit' means.

What we think we know and define as true in the 'real world' is nothing more than a transient agreement. Even as I write, the Darwinian theory of human evolution, Newtonian laws in physics and even Plank's & Einstein's theory of relativity, until now long standing absolutes in scientific and psychological thought, are being challenged by quantum leaps of discovery about the nature of sub-atomic particles ... even within our own brains.

Each of us can manifest the properties of a field of consciousness that transcends space, time, and linear causality.

Stanislav Grof (d.o.b. 01.07.1931), Psychiatrist
founder of the field of transpersonal psychology, *The Holotropic Mind*

It appears that there is more to us than we are permitted, or permit ourselves, to imagine. Learning to act questions the boundaries of what we think is possible. It stretches our boundaries and expands our imagination. In this light, it is not surprising that people ask me: 'Is this therapy?'

'Therapy' is not a very useful word in my book. There is a stigma attached to the word that implies there is something wrong with a person, as opposed to the society or environment they are living in.

There exist attitudes towards therapy, caring and teaching, where one could ask: 'Who are the insane?' One really only has to read Ron Johnson's hilarious, but rather sinister book, *The Psychopath Test*, to see that the official indicative characteristics of 'psychopathic behaviour' can just as easily describe a powerful world leader as they can someone who is incarcerated in Broadmoor Prison.

I mean, what are all these supposed human 'dis-orders'? Oppositional Defiant Disorder? Bipolar Disorder? Personality Disorder? General Anxiety Disorder? Attention Deficit and Hyperactivity Disorder? Attachment Disorder? Do we really know?

Could one not define these states of being or behaviours as 'Revolutionary', 'Pioneering', 'Magnetic', 'Artist', 'Activist', 'Actor', 'Philosopher', 'Leader' or, in the case of ADHD ... simply a 'Child'; a child healthily responding to the corruption and ignorance of the world around him/her? In some cultures these 'outsiders' are considered to be visionary.

Quite simply, the Playground cannot logistically, aesthetically or morally identify with all or any of the definitions that society currently uses as labels for 'mad', 'sane', 'normal' or 'abnormal' behaviour. If one wanted to, one could probably find sufficient evidence to postulate that we are all mad in some way.

No excellent soul is exempt from a mixture of madness

Aristotle, 384-322BC, Greek philosopher and scientist

I need to quickly add that I am completely aware that there are millions of brilliant parents, nurses, teachers, doctors and therapists, political activists, carers of all kinds, who are devoted to supporting those less informed or able than themselves, but whom are miserably unappreciated and underpaid. In fact, it is these wonderful people who are usually the ones who are most acutely aware of the need for more creative play in life/education, and who readily acknowledge its resuscitating effects upon themselves and those they care for.

The participants of the Playground are people who intuitively know that they are not everything they potentially can be or dream of being. They yearn for play and self-discovery. In that, they are all perfectly 'normal'.

I am talking about the vast majority of human-beings as they are born into the world, with the potential of *all things* within them, even the ones who have been told that they have some mentally or physically defined 'disorder' or who are clearly and understandably a bit shaky, wobbly or emotionally out of kilter in some way. There may be something that is temporarily challenging in their lives or about their behavioural personality, but very often all that's needed is a shift in conscious perception. Dramatic play provides that shift. It's as simple as that.

Growth as an actor and growth as a human being are synonymous.

Stella Adler, 1901-1992, American actress and teacher. *The Art of Acting*

Who Can Play?

The ages, experiences and backgrounds of those attracted to this type of play are extraordinarily diverse. In any typical group I might have a constellation of 6-9 very 'normal' and wonderful human-beings of mixed backgrounds, needs and abilities, all of whom want to learn to act and improvise. Some see it as a stepping stone towards entering the profession. The majority, however, simply sense that acting will empower them to become more self-expressive and socially more communicative and confident. They are of course completely correct in assuming this.

I'll be including some case studies of players later (with their generous permission and under their chosen pseudonyms). The following list of players represents a very small percentage of those whom I have encountered over the past forty odd years, but hopefully demonstrates the unpredictable dynamics and the all-inclusive nature of the Playgrounds I nurture:

- 35 year old journalist, who had reached a complete blank
- 37 year old single Mum, who wanted to do something for herself, finally
- 45 year old social worker who was depleted by the stress and trauma of social work
- 43 year old ex-policeman, ex-national health worker, turned Buddhist, who wanted to understand his emotions better
- 30 year old parcel force driver, who believed there had to be more to life than delivering consumer products to consumers in their homes
- 42 year old solicitor's clerk, who wanted to learn about comedy improvisation
- 22 year old working class lad, who dreams of making films

- 45 year old footballer, father of three kids, who felt he had lost touch with his playful side
- 38 year old self-employed male carpenter, who wanted to explore his/her identity and creative self-expression as a woman
- 40 year old language teacher, who wanted to use more drama and play in his teaching in the Middle East
- 46 year old computer expert, who was sick of communicating with a screen
- 50 year old woman with ME, who was trying everything to understand what is wrong with her, and doctors couldn't help
- 20 year old grocery shop worker, who very reticently talked about her childhood
- 35 year old, who started an acting career at 19, but ended up as a housewife
- 40 year old German anti-communist, anti-neo-Nazi revolutionary, who came out of hiding from East Berlin after the Wall came down. He organised my Playground sessions in the East Block

My groups have also included people with what are described as minor mental or major physical disabilities, for example 'autism'. As long as they, themselves, do not feel too disadvantaged or uncomfortable with everyone else in the group, it's totally up to them. Some, who are severely or temporarily physically disabled, are generally happy to sit and watch, joining in where or whenever they can. One can learn a lot from watching and observing. The general concept is that anyone can play if they want to. In short, I welcome the inclusion of mixed abilities, backgrounds and experiences, as we can all learn from each other.

There is only one clear restriction. I tend to stick to a rough lower age limit of 18 years. This is because the content of the sessions can get quite bawdy and dark sometimes. The games are catalysts for the shadowy, as well as the bright aspects of human-nature. Things happen that younger people might not appreciate or understand. Also, teenagers have a very real need to explore their imaginations and identities amongst their peers. Saying that, young people can be extraordinarily wise and mature for their age. But I have never included anyone younger than 18 years in my Playground sessions. Above that, there is no limit!

The Games

I have gathered other people's ideas along the way, as one does, through life and 50 years of acting and experiential play with players of all kinds in at least three different languages. Some of the games are based on well-known and recognisable children's games, the source of which can only be described as ancient. Others are based on 'classic' acting games that have emerged out of more recent experimental revolutions in theatre, which I have developed, given a surreal twist and renamed, with new clarifications as to what one can get out of them. I mention the origins, *if* I can remember where I first came across them! Many of the games in this book, however, are completely original. I know, because I made them up myself!

Ultimately the creative ideas I use have come about as a result of having spent a *lot* of time experiencing and witnessing their impact on players first hand. They are constantly evolving. I develop ideas for games all the time, adapting them as the situation arises, to meet the needs of the individual or the constellation of players that I'm playing with. Many of the games can be used over and over again in different ways, at various stages of discovery. But, no matter what relative level one wants to take these games to…just for fun, to stretch one's scope for survival on this beautiful, but unpredictable planet or for the purposes of professional development, my aim is to provide extremely diverse, playful and highly stimulating activities that can be sensually, physically, emotionally, mentally and mystically *experienced* and *observed*.

The Concepts

Through countless players experiencing and observing these games, discussions have arisen, which have inspired me to take a deeper look at what is actually taking place. Some of those discussions are expanded on in this book, but in the actual Playground I tend not to encourage too much theoretical dissection. Why try to analyse, justify or prove what is and what isn't, when the fact is we all have totally different explanations for the same things and words are often insufficient to describe what we feel or think we know.

> **When I use a word, it means just what I choose it to mean, neither more nor less."…said Humpty-Dumpty.**
>
> Lewis Carroll, 1832-98,
> *Through The Looking Glass, and What Alice Found There*

I personally don't think anything *needs* to be proven about the art of acting or playing or being human (in my experience, those three things are all pretty much the same thing) any more than proving that when you fill a glass to the brim and keep filling it, the water simply runs over the edge. The *act of doing it* proves it. Water everywhere! It's an I Ching sort of thing. If you take one course of action, this will happen. If you take another course of action, that will happen. And yet no *act*ion or re-*act*ion will ever be quite the same twice. Humans and animals don't obey the Newtonian laws that billiard balls seem to.

The simple truth, if there is a truth, is that there is more to life than we learn about in school and there's much more to us than meets the eye. If given permission, we can become something like magicians. We are *creative observers* and we possess something called *will-power*, which has not just the *potential* to change reality around us, but actually does, whether we intend it or not.

> **It appeared that the unconscious mind somehow had the capability of communicating with the sub-tangible physical world – the quantum world of all possibility. The marriage of unformed mind and matter would then assemble itself into something tangible in the manifest world**
>
> McTaggart, d.o.b. 1951, Journalist, Author, Publisher and Lecturer,
> *What the Doctor's Don't Tell You* and *The Field,* 2001:159

The paradoxical nature of who we really are and what we are capable of becomes more and more evident as we explore this acting dimension. Some describe it is a sort of shamanic zone that goes beyond the definitions of time, matter and space, but however one chooses to describe it, I am simply talking about humanity's very real ability to communicate in other ways, to inter-relate and connect mentally, sensually, intuitively and, above all, *empathically* ... to tune into the space and beings around us. There is something utterly essential and fascinating about this type of all-embracing play.

Ultimately, there is something fascinating and essential about you ... and that's what this game is all about. It's about YOU ... the essential, the eternal, the epiphany of YOU ... and the many MASKS you wear.

> **In the final analysis, we count for something only because of the essential we embody, and if we do not embody that, life is wasted.**
>
> C.G. Jung, 1875-1961, Swiss psychiatrist and psychotherapist,
> *Memories, Dreams and Reflections*, 1963:325

If you don't like what someone has to say, argue with them.   Noam Chomsky

CHAPTER TWO

PARALLEL WORLDS

ACTING FOR LIFE

I FIRST LEARNED to act consciously when I was 11 years old. Acting presented itself as a revolutionary escape from a world that was extremely confusing.

In the beginning ... life was great. I was a very lucky child indeed. Born into a Navel family in 1953, the year WW2 sweetie rations were lifted and Europe was shocked by Rock n' Roll, I travelled with my family around the circumference of planet Earth before I was the age of 10. In those early years, my imagination was well nourished with world wonders, bright sunlit colours and staggeringly beautiful scenery. I remember swimming with Maori children in the hot-springs in New Zealand. We travelled across America in a Cadillac. I remember the mists of the Niagara Falls falling on my cheeks and looking over the edge of a yellow-pink-red-orange canyon a mile deep. We drove through a giant Red Tree forest and I met real cowboys and Native American Indians. My ninth birthday was celebrated with a cake with white lemon icing on the banks of Snake Lake, just outside New York. Shortly after that I remember feeling my stomach plummeting to my feet in a super-fast lift up to the top of the Empire State Building. And I remember tough disciplinary love.

When I was 10 ... this was the confusing bit ... I was suddenly without warning sent to one of those horrendous red-brick Victorian institutions with long corridors, creaking floor boards and rows of metal-sprung beds with thin mattresses in dormitories supervised by ugly giant matrons in starched uniforms. It was a private boarding school for girls in Kent, far away from home. I was left there to fend for myself for a whole year. I was in complete shock and I can't say I did very well. For some reason, which I still don't understand, I was bullied badly. Any playful, imaginative precociousness was kicked, pinched and ridiculed out of me.

In retrospect, I learnt a lot from it. Later in life, it helped me empathise with people who are bullied, but at the time it was horrid. The repeated mockery, derision, torture and isolation reduced me to being a very weepy child that lost her memory. I had no idea why I was there, why the other girls chose to be mean to me, nor why the staff seemed oblivious of the fact that it was happening. I was so sad and lonely that I couldn't retain facts in my head anymore. I went from being classified 'a bright child' who, until that year, had been top of the class in most school subjects, to a child that failed almost everything.

Fortunately for me, after a year, my parents and my teachers agreed that there was something wrong with me ... not wrong with the schooling system, I hasten to add ... so they decided to place me in a day school closer to home.

I arrived at the new school on the first day, nervous, insecure and uncontrollably weeping over the tiniest thing. My new class mates nick-named me 'blubber box'.

But then I met Corky, who was something like a fairy godmother.

Joyce Corfield was an 'old pro' actress with blonde-grey fluffy hair, lipstick that travelled up the wrinkles around her mouth, face-powder that settled on her enormous bosom and earlobes that went purple because of the clip-earrings she always used to wear. She was the acting teacher at the new school and invited me to join her classes.

In short, she introduced me to everything I needed to know about acting. How to breathe. How to pause and suspend time. How to imagination myself into altered realities. I remember her asking me to go up on stage and be a talking tree. I sprang up, transformed into a weeping willow, told my story and grew invisible wings.

From then on, I was in my element. Cast in the main roles of the school plays, I passed my LAMDA exams with honours. If the reader doesn't know already, LAMDA exams, rather like piano or ballet exams, are the London Academy of Dramatic Art exams in acting skills, which are designed to qualify and prepare you for a potential career in acting.

I remember clearly the first time I heard thunderous applause and laughter. It was as if it was coming from another room, from outside this imaginative bubble I was in. There I was, 11yrs old, playing a mad old woman with a stuffed seagull on my hat. I was so enjoying what I was doing that I didn't consider for a moment that anyone would laugh or clap, but then I realised the applause was for me. Until that point I had had no idea that I could even be funny. I can't describe the elation I felt.

To be honest, I was extraordinarily lucky to have met Corky at that point of my life. Without her I would probably have ended up a mere ghost of myself. Either that or a violently angry child. Not only did she give me the basic skills to express myself imaginatively again, but she went out of her way to get permission for me to skip history, maths and geography lessons in order to rehearse the school plays! This would nowadays be unheard of.

My inner world of imagination rapidly expanded. When I wasn't making theatre, I spent a lot of time in the art studios, singing to myself and painting pictures all on my own ... instead of eating lunch. I won some art prizes and my parents thought perhaps I would choose to go to art school, but my heart was already devoted to the acting dimension. With theatre I knew I would be able to express myself in more ways than one; through multi-dimensional, living, breathing and moving pictures that involved movement, voice, poetry, music, costumes, make-up, stage sets and lighting design.

Perhaps more than anything else, through acting, I was becoming increasingly aware of the capabilities of the human mind. I became conscious of the art of illusion. I discovered the power of the Mask.

No-one spoke to me about the failings of the year before. It was as if it had never happened. In retrospect, I can see how this silence caused a psychological split in me to grow. A shadow was forming. My stage personas were growing more and more confident, but in the 'real world' of school uniforms, segregation of the sexes and out-dated text book knowledge, I was struggling to find an identity that had any real meaning. Nothing that my teachers said to me – apart from Corky – made any sense. I was intensely aware that what they said was contradictory to my inner experience of the world. There was no connection. It was as if people were lying to me or treating me as if I was stupid. When I contradicted them or expressed my curiosity, I was given to understand that I was 'being difficult' or 'trying to be clever'.

The only way I could retain any control over myself, that is who I was in the 'real' world, was to stop eating. Secretly. I began to lie. I said I was eating, when I wasn't. Everything else seemed to be beyond or out of my control. I became anorexic, which was ultimately something like a disappearing act or a cry for help. I, whoever I was, got skinnier and skinnier and wore more and more make-up, but still no-one seemed to notice or talk to me about the internal dilemma I was experiencing. I was just told to be quiet and behave. It was as if I didn't exist in the 'real world'. It was very strange.

It was the acting out of imaginary roles on stage that kept me sane and alive. Theatre gave me the option of expressing my inner self in artistic ways. It provided me with a very real dimension that was more colourful, expansive and meaningful than 'reality'. Heaven knows what traumatised young people do nowadays, when the arts are taken out of general education.

Throughout all the surreal ups and downs in my life (another book to be published at another time), it has been the acting dimension and the arts that have somehow held my inner and outer worlds together, creating a bridge between the two parallel realms, the 'visionary' and 'reality'. And it seems I have spent a life-time trying to understand and reveal the importance of the intimate relationship between these two parallel worlds. The inner and the outer. The Mask and the being behind the Mask.

To cut a long story short … After spending precious early years under Corky's wing, I was accepted, just 17 years old, skinny as a rake, at Bristol Old Vic Theatre School (B.O.V.T.S). I studied there for three intensive years (1971-4), married a Dane and moved to Copenhagen.

My career in professional acting didn't take off immediately, because I couldn't speak the language, so I decided to learn Danish as quickly as possible and, in the meantime, train in dance … and teach.

The Danes had a fantastic social system where, if you could find 12 people who were interested in learning the same thing, the government would pay the teacher good wages and the students could learn whatever they chose to learn at a greatly reduced cost. I found a lot of people who wanted to learn acting, or put it this way, they found me and each other. The majority were adults (21+ yrs) from differing backgrounds, who joined for a variety of reasons. Some wanted to enter the profession, others simply wanted to learn acting skills out of interest. So, by the age of 23, I was teaching acting skills to three different groups of 12 students every week in pigeon Danish.

My classes were, for whatever reason, popular. I wasn't sure why. I guessed it might have something to do with my personal style of teaching, which wasn't so much about teaching people to be 'stage-worthy', more about giving people permission to discover and express themselves freely, as Corky had done for me. I was teaching the professional techniques I had learnt at drama school, but was working from some kind of gut instinct about the benefits of human under-standing and non-competitive play. At that time, I didn't think about the *how's, why's* or *wherefores*. I was simply content that the classes were full and that all the participants were having a good time.

Suddenly, out of the blue, I got caught up in a whole chain of other dramatic events in my life. My professional work, now both in dance and theatre, took me to Paris for a year with an erotic dance company. Paradoxically, it was in the bohemian milieu of Paris that my understanding of the relationship between acting and ancient philosophies began.

I was introduced to the *I Ching*; the Taoist Book of Changes – specifically, the Richard Wilhelm translation with a forward by Carl Jung. I developed a fascination for the synchronistic play of mantic divination; how our unconscious knows things that our conscious mind doesn't seem to register.

At about the same time, I was also profoundly influenced by Ouspensky's book, *In Search Of The Miraculous*. Ouspensky writes about the Armenian philosopher George Ivanovich Gurdjieff (1866 – 1949) and his school of thought, and I remember reading that Gurdjieff spoke of acting as the 'highest human art form'.

All this was the beginning of a new level of consciousness for me, about the power of the acting techniques I was practicing. It became clear to me that these techniques gave me a greater ability to hold my *attention in the now* and an increased *awareness of choice* to follow either the superior or inferior parts of my nature – the spiritual or the animal, the rational or the intuitive, the sexual or the ascetic, the dark or the light.

After about a year in Paris (it was now 1979 and I was 26 years old), I was talent spotted and invited to work in Berlin. Within a year I was speaking some German and had become the 'star' of Berlin Night Life in a well-known cabaret venue called *La Vie En Rose*. The choreographer of the show gave me opportunities to explore and play with my identity in new ways. He supported me in dreaming up some unconventional cabaret acts, which got me a lot of media attention. I found myself entertaining V.I.Ps and celebrities like the Rolling Stones and Nina Hagen, as well as leading politicians, the British Forces stationed in Berlin, Deutsche Opera divas and some German T.V. entertainment stars. One thing led to another.

I ended up living in Berlin for about 17 years, going from one style of theatre to another, from Cabaret to Rock Theatre, Surreal Art performances to Cult-Films, as well as getting work in German State Theatre, Film and Television. Finally, I became a member of an English speaking fringe theatre company called the Berlin Play Actors. For eight years we explored classical plays. I was very lucky to be constantly in work, at times very 'successful', hitting front page news more than once. It was an absurd life, crazy and wonderful, but also quite schizophrenic.

On stage, I was playing a range of archetypical roles that were strong, deep, complex, outspoken and influential, and yet, in private, there was still this silent wounded-child inside me that quite often felt lost, vulnerable and insecure. I covered this vulnerability up with the Masks, alcohol and hard work. Looking back, I can see how a deepening of the split between my two parallel worlds, the inner and the outer, had to occur before I could begin to put it all together, before a real questioning of who 'I' really am and a 'What on earth am I doing?' could take place.

Once settled in Berlin, I advertised my teaching again, this time as coaching for professional actors. But again, people of all ages and backgrounds contacted me saying that they had *always wanted to know what acting was about*. Some wanted to get into professional theatre, but the majority were clear that they didn't want to become a professional actor. They told me they hoped that acting skills would somehow help them to become more confident. Some had had a taste of acting in school plays and loved it, others had had very bad experiences standing up in front of an audience when younger and knew that they must overcome this fear in order to progress in life.

Informed by my teaching experiences in Copenhagen, my gut instinct told me that they all simply wanted permission to be themselves – to be truly seen and heard, possibly for the first time in their lives. This period of time represented one of the biggest 'Aha' moments for me, in terms of who I am and the development of my teaching to what it has become now.

I began consciously realigning the repertoire of acting games and techniques that I used with the various philosophies I'd been studying. I made the whole process available in an accessible, funky kind of way, not to promote success in the *competitive professional arena*, but to address the needs of people who quite simply wanted to rediscover themselves and thereby become more creative and confident in LIFE.

I called the classes 'KUNST14'; a German title meaning ART14, which represented t*he alchemical marriage of the opposites* – the marriage of dualistic extremes and parallel worlds. I gave the players permission to go to the extremes of who they felt they were, to expose their as yet undiscovered genius, as well as their shadow; to express both the beautiful and the ugly, the comic and the tragic, in a safe sort of way.

In short, everyone had an absolute blast, doing some off the wall things, now and again accidentally hitting a point of emotional intensity and deep inner realisation, but always returning to cracking up with laughter and having some profound conversations about the puzzling and paradoxical nature of life in general.

Over the next 10-15 years in Berlin, I watched people's lives transform, including my own. The cathartic effects of joy, relief and increased clarity in the minds of the players were very apparent. The participants were all growing as human beings, becoming so much more expressive and honest and confident, less guilt ridden and apologetic, less self-absorbed and mistrustful, reaching out to care for others, sometimes completely re-organising their lives in positive ways for themselves and the people around them.

After the Berlin Wall came down in 1989, I was invited to cross over to the now open East sector to coach people who had literally been indoctrinated all their lives not to play, not to use their imaginations openly and not to express themselves in an individual or unique way. Again, using the techniques I was developing (that are case studied and described later in this book), I witnessed some profound transformations.

I began to document what I was doing. I developed more and more games, concepts and creative challenges for people to play with, rooted in the profes- sional techniques that I had learnt, but inspired by additional research, further training and my own general curiosity about the untapped imaginative potential of the human psyche.

This was, in fact, all just the beginning.

In 1995, circumstances lead me to leave Berlin and base myself in Devon, England, where I advertised my teaching once again. This time more specifically as A.C.T (Acting and Confidence Training) – an alternative approach to building confidence and self-belief through acting. Responses remained consistent and again I witnessed remarkable transformations. Ironically though, it was in the beautiful nature of Devon that I came to realise just how much of a virtual oasis I was offering people in a world that was globally becoming increasingly technological, finance driven, stressful and sedentary.

In 2000, I was offered a part-time job at a further education college for Performing Arts and Media, in Torquay, Devon. It was there that I began to comprehend the absurd complexities of working within the confines of an 'educational institution' with its government controlled outcomes and criteria. I was not considered 'qualified' to teach as such, so the college invited me to complete a CertEd-FE (Certificate of Education for Further Education) i.e. a teaching qualification, which is now the equivalent of a PGCE (Post Graduate Certificate of Education). The government were funding these courses at the time, so the training was free, which was great! During the three years that I studied at the college, in conjunction with the training, I taught performing arts at HND (Higher National Diploma) and BTEC (Business and Technology Education Council) levels. I was tutoring classes of c. 25 teenagers, between the ages of 16-19 years old!

Teaching performing arts to young people should be a very rewarding job. But, it wasn't. Ridiculous amounts of monitoring, evaluations, paper work, over-filled classes and a sudden Ofsted Inspection resulted in pure stress for everyone, teachers and pupils alike. Fun was sadly sporadic. In short, pointless amounts of hard work for very little pay. I was expected to work three hours for every paid hour. I found myself working overtime to the point of mental exhaustion, with very little effect. It was like herding reluctant animals to a market.

Despite the exasperating stress of it all, I did gain a lot from the teacher training course itself. I was intrigued by the concept of *facilitating* learning (making it easier to learn), while at the same time being utterly bemused by the irony of the impossibility of facilitating anything at all in such a stressful environment. I became fascinated with studying different forms of psychology and philosophy in this context. In particular, the works of the American psychologist Abraham Maslow (1908–1970) caught my attention with his *Hierarchy of Human Needs*.

Human beings have an innate tendency to move toward higher levels of health, creativity and self-fulfilment

Abraham Maslow, 1908-1970,
Motivation and Personality, 1970, 3rd edition

I began consciously formulating my own opinions about the indisputably vital role of curiosity and creative play in a human's drive towards self-actualisation. Being at that time particularly afflicted by *abnormal stress levels*, which seemed to be everywhere I looked in the working world around me, especially within the educational system, it became horrifically clear to me that the *innate tendency* that Maslow spoke of was being seriously thwarted by the educational system itself. Indeed, the red alert stress levels at that college eventually got the better of me too. After three years I quit the job, as did many of my forerunners for the same reason.

The cripplingly stressful environment I experienced in this 'educational institution' (and I am sure that this was/is typical of many other such institutions) awakened in me an urgent need to study the psychology of learning in relation to *cognitive/behavioural* approaches, *creative play, imagination* and *communication skills*. I went on to complete a one year pre-diploma certificate in Humanistic (Person Centred) Counselling and then became a Master Practitioner of Neuro Linguistic Programming (NLP) in 2004. After that I completed another one year pre-diploma certificate in Clinical Hypnosis, which in turn led to other things.

In 2005, I was employed by the Peninsula Medical School (PMS) to use acting and role-play to train medical students in advanced communication skills. I continue to work there to this day, I am honoured to say, as it is a pioneering form of training that reveals much about the essential healing powers of empathic listening and its relevance in excellent communication.

In case the reader is not familiar with what this type of role-play work is, I will briefly explain. My creative task at PMS is to act out the role of a simulated patient, presenting their symptoms with a given case history of a mental and/or physical disorder. The medical student interviews me as a doctor would a patient in a regular G.P. clinic, after which I step out of role and facilitate the student's understanding of his/her interviewing techniques with regards to his/her ability to *create rapport, gather relevant information* and *empathise* with the patient.

What is lesser known is that *empathy* and *listening* are not just essential qualities in any healing relationship, but also, in fact, two top professional acting techniques (I will be discussing these techniques in much greater depth in Chapters 4 and 5).

Gradually, over the past two decades, it has become clear to me that the knowledge and skills I have as an actor have strong correlations with modern break-through paradigms in the fields of communication, psychology, psychic research, medicine and neuroscience. In fact, what I have observed, and this is really important, is that skilled actors tend to quite naturally and intuitively understand much about psychology, body language and the workings of the human mind, in comparison with psychologists, doctors, teachers, neurologists, scientists and nurses, who don't seem to know much about acting techniques ... if anything at all.

As a precursor to some of what is to come in the rest of the book, I'd like to briefly give a couple of examples of the type of correlations I have observed:

1. NEURO LINGUISTIC PROGRAMMING (NLP) is practiced widely these days in the contexts of CBT (cognitive/behavioural therapy), corporate training, life-coaching and personal development. Many people think it is some kind of weird, cult form of 'brain washing', probably because the name suggests that, which is unfortunate. In my experience, NLP is not only one of the fastest, most positive, non-invasive methods of bringing about personal transformation, but even more importantly offers practitioners and explorers very modern, progressive tools and techniques for excellent communication.

NLP introduces the idea that we are all *wired* neurologically in different ways, plus the idea that we all have our own installed patterns, programmes, memories and visions. Each of us has a unique way of assimilating and interpreting the world around us. Therefore, we each perceive 'reality' differently, which is something that people very often don't realise or forget, when arguing their own point of view. We think that other people *should* be able to see things the way we see them. Consequently, one of NLP's primary presuppositions is: *'The map is not the territory.'* Let me elucidate.

If a Native American, a Tourist and a Lumber Jack were all to draw their own maps of the same forest, then their three maps would probably look completely different, with different signs, symbols and points of interest. The best way to get to know someone is therefore not to presume that their map is the same as yours, but to *discover what their map looks like.*

In acting, it is similar. We have to see and feel things from other peoples' perspectives. We have to *walk a mile in another person's shoes* in order to get inside the mind, body, head, voice, feelings, sensations, experiences and inner motivations of the role we wish to play. We *empathise.* We tune into and become, in some way, one with another person.

2. THE SHADOW. The idea of the opposite or the double within the human psyche was introduced into the field of psychology by the famous Swiss psychiatrist and psychotherapist Carl Jung (1875-1961). I will be referring to this concept (and other aspects of his teachings) in more detail later, as an awareness of the Shadow is an integral part of the empowerment of any player who plays in the Playground. With the Shadow we encounter the extremes of good and potential evil that exist within us all. This too is the work (or play) of an actor. Understanding the Shadow and its impact is fundamentally a search for the 'truth' of a role or indeed the complexities of who that person can be.

I personally am not sure in what order of events I began to become conscious of my Shadow. I only relatively recently began to study Jung's works in more depth. It seems that the Shadow has always been a part of my dreams and my reality, from a young age. Working in theatre all my life has meant that I have regularly encountered and explored the shadowy or hidden aspects of human nature, my own included. The tragic, the dark, the demonic, the undesired, the fearful, the suppressed and the taboo are clearly depicted in great literary works, such as Shakespeare's *Macbeth*, and in theatre's many mirrored reflections of the world around us, ancient and modern. In fact, one could say that in various theatrical contexts (those that are is not censored for political or educational reasons) the Shadow is central and openly portrayed ... just as it is quite naturally embraced in the Playground and, thanks to Jung, in any informed psychological encounter.

As we progress into the heart and underbelly of the Playground, we will see how EMPATHY and the SHADOW, intertwine beautifully with other acting concepts and techniques that I have not yet elaborated on e.g. IMAGINATION, the MASK, WHO I AM IS WHAT I SEE and THE CREATIVE GAZE (Chapter 4 and 5). Together they form a dynamic meta-physical formula for human understanding and transformation.

There is one other ingredient that I want to mention now; something that is not automatically associated with acting and is difficult to speak about or even name. It is one of those invisible elements of the acting dimension that is undeniably present and tangible for anyone to feel, sense and experience, if they choose. It is a tricky subject.

Transcendence

Spirituality, mysticism and transcendence are controversial words that tend to trigger a kind of domino effect in some people's minds, rapidly forming associations with religious beliefs and practices, fundamentalism, cults and radical forms of exclusivity, which I personally don't have anything to do with.

For me an experience of transcendence is simply an indication of an ability to sense the existence of something greater or other than ones physical biological being; some kind of energy that one can somehow connect with it, tune into and be a part of.

Some modern scientists call this invisible energy the Field [The Quantum Field of Sub-Atomic Information]. Pioneering minds in the Victorian era proposed it is Vortex Energy. Quantum physicists believe that everything is energy, therefore humans and objects are as well. Others prefer to separate humans from this invisible energy and name it God, Allah, the Tao, Chi or (in its plural form) Elohim. Whatever 'it' is, feminine or masculine, singular or plural, or all these things at once, one might be able to agree that it is something like *an energy* that seems to permeate everything and could be the source of everything. If you take it away, the structure of what we believe exists will fall apart. We all have different perceptions, so I am very careful about questioning anyone's belief system or preferred scientific theory. It is a vast subject and only a closed mind can be certain.

However, I feel a few observations made by various Playground players in this context can't easily be ignored.

In 2005, a few Buddhist practitioners were attending my classes on a regular basis, and I was surprised when they told me that learning to act was similar to certain Buddhist concepts and practices.

> **I have been meditating for five years and never got so close to myself and my real physical being as with this Acting thing ... Acting is totally experiential in a way meditation can never be and yet it touches on the same knowledge. This is extra-ordinary stuff ...**
>
> Player's testimony

I had never studied Buddhism, being a bit of a fool and part-time Taoist myself, but when I discussed these observations with them in more depth, I came to realise that both acting and meditation have the potential to lead the individual towards:

- *a mind/body awareness, where one's self is a witness to one's own actions*
- *a greater ability to maintain attention in the now*
- *increased emotional intelligence*
- *a consciousness of the whole spectrum of one's being; the light, as well as the dark*
- *a consciousness that one is part of something greater than oneself*

> **Once you have understood the basic principle of being present as the watcher of what happens inside you – and you understand it by experiencing it – you have the most potent transformational tool.**
>
> Eckhart Tolle, d.o.b. 1948, *The Power of Now*, 1999:34

I will be describing games, creative challenges and techniques where these types of phenomena might be experienced, not as proof of its existence, but as examples of contexts where the feeling of *transcendence* or this 'out of body experience' may occur … if one chooses to see it in this way. But not everyone does. We see what we want to see or believe we can see. It's complex.

Typically acting is thought of as a glamorous profession that is rather narcissistic, licentious and profane. On certain levels, it is. I can't deny it. Theatre is like a hall of mirrors that reflects the irreverently debauched, as well as the intimately sacred. Certainly the relevance of box office profits (commercial success) has brought out both the best and worst in practitioners of this ancient art form since the beginning of time.

In the beginning, because of my lack of clarity about who 'I' was, I mistakenly used the hook of a potential career in the glamorous world of acting as a sort of carrot to inspire the players to develop their expressive abilities further. Just as the profession had done for me. Although I respected that many entered the Playground with absolutely no wish to enter the acting profession at all, I observed that once they discovered they *could* act, there was of course the inevitable lure of 'success' in the business. Some players have indeed gone on to use those skills to make money in the profession. But, there was this incongruity that nagged my conscience on an unconscious level; an on-going split in my being that was playing tricks on me.

At some point I began to realise that 'I', whoever I was, was functioning in two separate worlds. On the outer surface the Mask flirted dangerously with the world around me, playing the game, as it were, of 'success' in the profession. Behind the Mask, behind closed doors, in private relationships, I was the 'real me'; the insecure, vulnerable me that allowed myself to be abused, bullied and trampled all over.

Two very different beings, with different voices, desires and opinions. The Mask was confidently popular and 'successful', but the being that created the Mask, behind it, chose not to speak openly. And yet the two were intimately connected. I knew this. The acting techniques I had learnt in my early years and at drama school had given me this knowledge.

I had to ask myself, who was this silent spirit that existed behind the Mask? This being that was so creative and observant and yet so shy? Crucially, I had to ask myself, how was I able to support other people in the learning of life skills through acting, when I myself felt so insecure about who 'I' really was in 'real life'?

Then suddenly, in that strange synchronistic way, another student of mine told me about a teacher of Dharma in the East, who had suggested that *acting is likely the easiest profession to awaken through.*

Now, this was a really interesting point … simple and clear … leading to one of the central principles of my teaching now. I know what this wise man is saying. I agree, and disagree. Yes, learning to act professionally can certainly be empowering and extremely informative about the complex condition of being human. It gives one highly expressive tools for creative communication and transformation. It introduces one to self-awareness and the power of imagination. It awakens one to one's creative potential.

BUT ... why should it be necessary to enter the *profession* in order to gain access to this knowledge?!

This is the crux of it.

In my opinion, contradictory to what some top teachers and elite practitioners of this art form claim, acting is not a god given gift that only a few possess. It is an innate ability that we are born with. As children we model, mirror, imitate and re-act to the world around us. We imagine. We dream. We invent. We create. We play. We feel. We connect. This is essentially what acting is. It is just that, at some point in time, we are told to stop misbehaving ... Stop day dreaming. Stop showing off. Stop mucking about. Stop playing up. Stop imagining that you are something you are not. Stop crying. Stop being emotional. We become confused. We retreat into a shell. Our precious gift disappears into the shadows.

Sadly, understanding and refining the art of acting i.e. taking these innate abilities to another consciously creative, mature and confidently expressive level, normally involves some kind of ambitious and expensive career choice ... to enter the *acting profession*.

I will be exploring this blind spot in more detail in Chapter 3: *Invisible Walls*, but first I would like to try to summarise what it is like at the top end of the market, in this highly coveted and exclusive *profession* ... or at least, how I experienced it.

The Acting Profession

There is so much competition in the acting business, so many people who desire to be an 'actor' that only a few get into the top academies in London, USA and Europe, which is where the coveted acting secrets are taught. And it's not getting easier as populations rise.

If you do get in, the training is rigorous and demanding, both physically and mentally. This has to be so, firstly because of the very nature of acting, which engages every aspect of your mind, body and spirit, but also because one needs to be prepared for the extreme competitiveness in the global market place, where looking the part, brand manipulation, money and 'success' go hand in hand.

One could argue that the business itself is, in fact, the *real* training ground. It is there that you are really tested. It is there that you come up against the shadow side of glamour and human nature. Look at the state of the arts. TV Reality Shows, Soap Operas, Block Buster Films, Commercial Theatre and

Consumer Ads, bespattered with glittering celebrity culture, sponsored by dubious advertising and political propaganda strategies. Although creatively playful and exciting, it can be equally superficial, corrupt, stressful and, to be honest, main stream and plain boring. It is hard to imagine how one could be 'awakened' in such an environment.

'Success' is great, of course, and is usually financially rewarding. But ironically, at the end of the day, you might have to accept that the criterion for your 'success' in the eyes of the industry, peers, public and press, might well be that *you earn a lot of money, your face is recognisable and you have white teeth.* If you don't, and it isn't, you've failed. It is as simple as that. You're at the mercy of everyone else's judgement of 'success', not your own.

One of the main aims, therefore, of recognised theatre academies, is to prepare you for this rigorous test. The training streamlines the chosen students into a market that requires a particular style and image, incorporating not just an ability to show emotions easily, to be open and vulnerable, but also an ability to be tough skinned and marketable too.

The lucky few that complete a top training, may well find themselves unintentionally or intentionally complicit in the choice of entering a rather Machiavellian world, where only the exceptionally talented, well-connected, rich or extremely ambitious, eccentric and persevering have the slenderest chance of survival, let alone 'success'. If you have the slightest physical or mental weak-ness, if you are 'too old' or if you quite simply don't have the right attitude, stamina, looks or luck i.e. if someone else, similar to you, gets there first, you probably won't get the job. All of this requires the wit, guile, bravery, guts, psychic intelligence and constitution of a prostitute and a magician. If you've got all of that, then I agree you might be something like an 'awakened' being.

What I'm saying is that the acting *profession*, although it offers many glamorous rewards, does not necessarily promise you integrity, truth, the development of consciousness or spiritual awakening as such. The line between being in control of one's career and allowing oneself to be prostituted for commercial interests or the allure of 'success' (whatever that is) is like balancing on a treacherous knife edge, which some master and some don't. I personally walked on that edge many times myself and I didn't always get it right. No wonder I was often feeling split and confused about who 'I' really was.

Please do not mistake me. I am very grateful to have been spotted as talented. I am eternally grateful for the career opportunities that were given to me. I was lucky. Very lucky. I got well paid jobs on recommendation. One thing always led to another but, I knew there was more to life than this career. In between the highs I found myself seriously questioning the reality that I was exposed to. My answers have brought me to where I am now.

My vision is that many more people, in particular adults who educate, manage, train and care for others, should be able to benefit from learning the best acting techniques, without having to necessarily compete in the profession. It is, after all, not as if one is stealing magicians' tricks.

So, what are these illusive techniques that actors learn about in top academies and in the profession?

The following brief summary is by no means an extensive representation of everything that is out there. I mention these names and concepts purely because these are the ones I personally would recommend researching if anyone is interested:

There's Constantin Stanislavski's System with his imaginative *as if, truth* and *sense memory* concepts; Michael Chekhov, with his understanding of the nature of imagination and the *creative gaze*; Jerzy Grotowski with his demanding physical discipline in search of the *essential*; Antonin Artaud with his vision of Alchemical Theatre as opposed to the materialistic superficiality of Western civilization; Augusto Boal with his Forum Theatre techniques and devotion to social change; Jacob Levy Moreno with his science of Truth and his statement that *'God is spontaneity'*; Declan Donnellan, with his concept *'Who I am is what I see'* and the inevitable dynamics between *opposites* in life; Peter Brook with his rejection of 'deadly theatre' and his eye for the invisible space between things; Sanford Meisner, the method acting teacher who said: *'acting is the art of self-revelation'* [Meisner & Longwell 87:162]; Stella Adler who said:*'the most important thing the actor has to work on is his [her] mind'*; Viola Spolin and her vision of a world of *accessible intuition* [Spolin 1999:xi]; and finally Keith Johnstone with his hilariously refreshing ideas for improvisation and reflections on human behaviour in general.

There are many philosophies about acting, many different bibles that claim to be the most insightful and, as with various religions in the world, they are indeed all brilliant and valid in some way. For me there is no separation between them. In my mind, all the differing schools of thought, ancient and modern, essentially complement and overlap each other beautifully and, if we don't make the mistake of becoming too fixated on the one or the other, there is certainly a fascinating wisdom to be gained from all of them.

I will be referring to some of these practitioners again later and explaining their techniques in more detail, demonstrating with case studies and examples of games, how they relate to essential life skills, how they can empower us and enhance our view of ourselves as creative beings with unique gifts that we can give the world.

To conclude this chapter, let me summarise how I personally relate to my life in this playful acting dimension ... how I see things now.

In Greek 'Theatron' means *place where you view*. Since the beginning of recorded history, theatre has been used as a place to observe human behaviour; to play, mirror, inspire and ritualise social, political, cultural change; to witness human transformation. Theatre … and therefore I presume acting, as the actor is central to all theatre and ceremonial ritual, either as priest, shaman, magician, king/queen, politician or member of a chorus … is ancient. 5000 years old or more? Probably older. 10,000 years? What do we really know? As far as we know, the Islamic religion is c. 1,400 yrs old. Buddhism is c. 2,500 years old. Christianity not much older. How long have humans inter-*act*ed on this planet? 100,000+ years? We know as much as we can measure with the scientific recording devices that we have so far imaginatively created. We know what we imagine.

No matter where we look, we find this creative drive throughout our evolution; the art of imaginatively reinventing our stories and reinventing who we are in relationship to the world around us. As we did when we were children.

Today, we see theatre all around us… in theatre royals, music venues, vaudeville and burlesque clubs, amateur dramatic societies, street entertainment, arts festivals, holiday camps, football stadiums, dance events, Olympic arenas, cinemas, arts therapy groups, corporate development workshops, courts of law, lecture halls, Ted talks, the Houses of Parliament, churches, cathedrals, mosques, not forgetting the dramatic rituals (and scandals) in the palaces of Kings and Queens.

In addition to these more obvious outlets, one has to acknowledge that being a teacher, a nurse, a doctor, a policeman or manager of people, a politician in the modern world i.e. performing convincingly and effectively in any profession, involves human communication. Good communication requires good, if not excellent acting skills.

Understanding the disciplines and intricacies of self-expression seems to be central to cultural change and key to human survival. Put it this way, there are very few people who *don't* want to know what acting is all about! They recognise it as being key to some sort of power. And yet (I will be exploring this in the next chapter) there are very few opportunities to learn these essential life skills, other than in a competitive and exclusive market arena.

Even where the benefits of these mysterious things called *acting skills* are gradually becoming more globally recognised as essential human resources … by which I mean *cognitive/behavioural techniques, role-play, mirroring, emotional intelligence, lateral thinking (thinking outside the box) and 'fake it to make it' concepts*, all of which certainly support powerful presentation skills and excellence in achievement … they are currently being introduced into the corporate world with the aim of enhancing persuasive tactics and team building to promote the growth of big business agendas. Which is good, if the business aims are humane and environmentally friendly.

I personally am not interested in coaching people in powerful acting skills in order to promote the sales of completely unnecessary consumer products, nor to enhance suspect corporate or capitalist marketing tactics, nor to support the work of heartless big bankers, nor to persuade people that they can be rich and famous. I have a different definition of 'success'. One is not rich because one has a lot, one is rich because one doesn't need much. A child doesn't need expensive toys to play with.

Where are the boundaries between the logical reality we think we live in and the eternal vastness of our imaginative mind and intuitive feelings? Who creates those boundaries? Which part of us is relating to which part of whose dream?

> **All the world's a stage,**
> **And all the men and women merely players:**
> **They have their exits and their entrances;**
> **And one man in his time plays many parts,...**

Shakespeare, *As You Like It* 2/7

Life is an Act, a Play, a Game, a Dream, if one permits oneself to see it as such. Equipped with the right knowledge and seen from another perspective, the rules of the game can change. It becomes a game that we can all play.

CHAPTER THREE

INVISIBLE WALLS

BEFORE I DESCRIBE the games and techniques that I use, I need to take the reader on what might initially seem to be a rather boring, discursive tangent. We need to go back to school again. Sorry. I will be as brief as possible, but it's incredibly important. In fact, I believe this chapter will be surprisingly engaging for many readers; certainly for those who have experienced a standard British public or grammar school education.

I am going to take a critical and challenging look at what's really out there in terms of opportunities for the 'average punter' (let's call him/her Sam Brown for now) to learn acting skills as s/he grows up in the world. I want to demonstrate what is crucially missing and why Playgrounds, or oases of this nature, are desperately needed despite the apparent abundance of dramatic openings on offer.

Some of my arguments might seem obvious or even contradictory to the story I have told about my life so far, but the truth is that what I experienced was very unusual. Corky was a diamond and I was very fortunate to meet her when I did.

How do I know this?

I have heard the stories of hundreds of players' lives and shared their childhood experiences. In doing so, I have identified some major barriers that prevent people from empowering themselves through the study of acting techniques. Apart from the most obvious hurdle i.e. that of gaining entry into the acting profession itself, which I have already discussed, there are three other barriers that are less obvious, but which seriously undermine one's belief that one can or even has the right to learn about acting (which, as we will gradually discover, is about *being one's self*): *The Traumas of Institutionalisation; Ignoring the Child Within;* and *Feelings of Separation.*

The Traumas of Institutionalisation

> **Children do not have to be taught to be curious. But they may be taught, as by institutionalisation, NOT to be curious.**
>
> Abraham Maslow 1970:24

Looking back over the forty years that I have been enabling people to express themselves more freely and thus regain self-belief and a form of coherence back into their lives, I can safely say that the most reoccurring cause of emotional trauma (greater perhaps than childhood abuse, poverty, neglect, bullying, a fractured family, war or unexpected 'shock' disasters) stems from school education. Unspeakable damage is done by *the way we are taught* and, even more so, by the limiting things we are expected to learn about in school and accept as truth.

Not all schools are bad. Some are inspired and very successful at producing students not just with good exam results, but with a compassionate vision and the integrity, backbone and strength to go out and change the world in positive ways.

Certainly, there are thousands of brilliant teachers, working a fifty hour week for a pittance, who devote their energy to directing young people towards new brighter horizons. And there are millions of children all over the world, who would give their right arm for those opportunities.

I suppose one could say that the study of any form of knowledge is a privilege and should be valued as such, but, in my mind, the question arises: 'What knowledge?' 'What are we being forced to learn and why?', 'And who decides this?'

When I talk about damage, I am referring to standard compulsory education in what we consider to be 'normal' schools in Western societies, where classes are overfilled and where the individual's real gifts are more often than not neglected, ignored or suppressed.

It seems that the sole objective of academically streamlining (indoctrinating) the individual is to prepare them for an already saturated, overpopulated and, let's face it, greedily competitive consumer's market (or whatever the next social construct is on the political agenda). We are forced by law into an education that strives to make us ignorant of our human rights as free thinking individuals and of our true potential. We are groomed into working in a highly stressful environment that calls itself a democracy, but where governmental decisions that affect all of us are made long before they come to a public vote. Our lives are determined for us, without us even being aware of it.

This is the type of traumatic damage I am referring to. Predictions for the chaos we are now experiencing were made already a century and a half ago.

We must do away with the absolutely specious notion that everybody has to earn a living. It is a fact today that one in ten thousand of us can make a technological breakthrough capable of supporting the rest. The youth of today are absolutely right in recognizing this nonsense of earning a living. We keep inventing jobs, because of this false idea that everyone has to be employed at some kind of drudgery because, according to Malthusian-Darwinian theory, he must justify his right to exist. So we have inspectors to inspect inspectors. The true business of people should be to go back to school and think about

whatever it was they were thinking about before somebody came along and told them they had to earn a living.'
Richard Buckminster Fuller, 1895-1983. American
neo-futuristic architect, systems theorist, author, designer and inventor

Now, of course, there are not enough jobs to go around and we are spending billions on research into the potential of robots! Madness. Some seem to thrive in this competitively academic, but sedentary climate that is in fact a form of slavery. Many more clearly don't. Many don't want to compete to excel in subjects that lead them to places they don't want to go and mean nothing to them at all.

If a government or a school *really* wanted each and every growing individual to self-actualise and thrive, as they imply they do, physically, mentally and emotionally, to be truly motivated and to know what they want or can do best in life, then they would, first of all, make sure that there are no more than 10-12 children in one class, that good teachers are well paid and that all teachers would have a basic understanding of acting and the need for creativity.

Secondly, they would provide far more resources for the arts, as arts in general clearly *engage the heart, the senses and the imagination* of all beings and enhance all aspects of learning. I don't mean just in primary schools and kinder-gartens, but at all levels of learning. When I say 'engaging the heart', I mean *emotionally, empathically and sensually*. I mean that we must stimulate the feelings and the senses of young people through creative and imaginative play. Far too often, schools attempt to engage the heart through aerobic sports and dance activities, in order to counter obesity and diabetes. Physical exercise is excellent (I know this, I learnt to dance), but what about the emotions that are also stored, often trapped in the body? We must encourage people to be in touch with their emotions, by engaging with their inner imaginative world and devel-oping a more *intuitive* understanding of themselves and others in the world around them. Imagination manifests in a universal symbolic language. We call this language art, music, poetry, architypes, myths and dreams. It is here we discover that all human-beings on the planet are one. In this dimension we all speak the same language.

Thirdly, they would make *learning to act* an essential subject in any curriculum, not just as an option towards a career choice in theatre, but as a means of exploring imagination and thereby developing self-confidence, self-expression, empathy, emotional intelligence, communication skills and human understanding in any walk of life.

In short, learning to act and improvise is a complete body workout; physical and mental. It engages the whole anatomy, the spine, the nerves, the senses, the brain and the emotional heart strings. Even at a very basic level it develops at least sixteen vital human abilities: *imagination, memory, self-awareness, self-belief, creative-expression, language, understanding of body-language, emotional intelligence, intuition, self-direction, attention, motivation, active listening, communication skills, balance, presence, empathy and human understanding ...*

Let us now take a look at what opportunities there are for Sam Brown, as s/he grows up in the world, to learn these acting skills?

Many would argue that the majority of schools offer this kind of play already, in the form of theatre. In some ways they are right. Using forms of drama, forum theatre, improvisation and spontaneous role-play in a learning context is not completely new. Many mainstream schools in Britain (hopefully increasingly so) incorporate much more play and theatre into learning than they did half a century ago, when I went to school. The benefits of T.I.E (Theatre in Education) are now more commonly recognised thanks to a project undertaken, by the Belgrade Theatre in Coventry in 1965. Apparently, what the Belgrade Theatre company did was put some of the students, dressed as Native American Indians, into a cage and then got the other students, dressed as cowboys, to discuss the situation. They encouraged the young people through role-play to *see things from a different perspective.*

This is certainly a much more fun and stimulating way of discovering interesting human truths than the old fashioned Victorian method of sitting in rows and being lectured at by a teacher with a cane behind his back.

One needs to be aware, however, that professional practitioners of T.I.E don't teach *acting and improvisation techniques as such*. That is not their aim. The primary goal of T.I.E is to facilitate the learning of set curricular mainstream subjects, using theatrical devising, role play and discussion as tools to draw the students into a more direct experience of the subjects they are expected to learn.

What's missing here is a more in depth knowledge of what acting is really about.

So, in what other way or context can Sam Brown learn about the heavily guarded secrets of the acting profession?

If Sam is a natural talent, s/he may unconsciously tune into a few precocious tricks in the ubiquitous primary school Nativity Play. Little Sam could play the donkey or, if s/he's lucky, be cast as Mary or Joseph or one of the three Kings bearing gifts from the East or even ... the Star! Baby Jesus is usually played by a doll.

There's the possibility of learning some very basic acting skills in secondary school drama productions of 'Oliver Twist' or 'Grease', where young Sam *might* get a part if s/he proves her/himself extrovertly talented enough.

Outside of school hours, if Sam comes from a more wealthy family, there are the franchised stage schools, with their 'jazz hands' approach for potential young starlets of musical theatre. One might also be lucky to find an ambitious Youth Drama Group in the local community that organises opportunities for youngsters to get involved with professional entertainment projects and take the London Academy of Dramatic Art (LAMDA) exams.

As a career choice in school, Sam could move on to GCSE, BTEC and A Levels in the Performing Arts. If young Sam does well in all these things, is committed and considered gifted, if s/he is not intimidated into submission or introversion by either academic or peer pressures or poor acting tuition, s/he could then go on to apply for a place in a university drama department or, like myself, an acting academy. But, as I warned in the last chapter, even if s/he is highly talented, Sam Brown's chances of getting into a top academy, where the real acting techniques are taught, are statistically highly unlikely.

The vast majority of young adults enter the job world with a very simplistic understanding of what acting techniques actually are, even though they would be extremely useful in almost any walk of life.

In fact, what I have found, when sharing childhood learning experiences with adult non-actors, is that a lot of serious psychological and emotional damage is done when a sensitive child is taught stage crafts in the wrong way i.e. is expected to stand up in front of an audience and perform, without understanding how. The trouble being that the average classroom teacher doesn't understand how to do it either!

The worst case scenario is when a nervous child is exposed to the most common disciplinary acting directions of *'speak louder!'*, *'face the audience'*, *'stand in the spotlight'*, *'you haven't learnt your lines yet'* and *'you need to believe in your character'*, all-be-it in some ways appropriate in the majority of theatrical contexts, but actually brutally Dickensian. This form of acting tuition represents a terrifying prospect for those that don't get it or can't do it or for those that are simply too introverted or shy to believe in themselves, let alone the character they are supposed to be playing!

Also, because of current modern associations with the glamour of 'stardom' and celebrities in the T.V., film and acting world, school productions often engender a feeling of separation or failure in those who don't know *how* to perform confidently in front of an audience, or who were not chosen to play a main role, because you see, if you are an actor, you're a 'star'!

My heart simply goes out to all the other little stars; the ones in the shadows; the ones that are too afraid to shine ... or don't even *want* to shine in such a conventionally commercial and superficial way.

But what other option do we have, other than to try to fit in?

Children, historically, have rarely been given much *choice* in the things they are told to do and learn in life. Some of us have had great childhoods, but we should not play blind to the fact that child abuse in many forms, including forced labour and sexual trafficking is rampant all over the globe and finances some of the biggest and most corruptly flourishing capitalist industries. Children cannot change this, but as we become adults, as we become more independent, aware of what is going on, and can make our own choices in the world, as we become more conscious of the things that are missing in our lives, there are a few options out there for radical change and transformation.

For example, learning to act.

Ignoring the Child Within

> **To adjust well to the world of reality means a splitting of a person. It means that the person turns his back on much in himself because it is dangerous. But it is now clear that by doing so, he loses a great deal, too, for these depths are also the source of his joys, his ability to play, to love, to laugh, and, most important for us, to be creative.**
>
> Abraham Maslow 1970:24

Time and time again, I have heard the same stories about how people were unable to pursue their dream of learning to act. They describe how they loved it when they were younger, but found themselves caught up in a very basic 9-5 existential survival, serving a system that is dysfunctional, living a life of making ends meet by running faster and faster around some kind of an absurd treadmill. They ask me: 'Am I too old to learn to act?'

There is no doubt in my mind. One is never too old to dream, to play, to learn to improvise and to get in touch with the inner child again. One is never too old to develop one's imagination and transform.

> **(Neuroplasity is) ... the brain's ability to reorganize itself by forming new neural connections throughout life. Neuroplasticity allows the neurons (nerve cells) in the brain to compensate for injury and disease and to adjust their activities in response to new situations or to changes in their environment.**
>
> MedicineNet.com

Neuroplasticity is a bit of a buzz word, currently discussed amongst Western neuroscientists/psychologists and Eastern spiritual teachers of meditation. It has been shown that meditation stimulates neuroplasticity. I propose that learning to act does this too. Let me explain a bit more about this not so recent discovery.

Mark Rosenzweig (1922-2008) was an American researcher, who found that if laboratory rats were given a rich and stimulating environment, with play wheels and toys, they developed larger brains than those kept in a bare cage. I strongly oppose the use of animals in scientific experiments, but at least in this case some of the rats were given fun toys to play with.

> **Through extensive studies of this phenomenon at UC Berkeley in the 1950s and '60s, Rosenzweig and his colleagues were able to show that "environmental therapy" can stimulate brain growth at a cellular level not only in children, but also in adults i.e. the brain continues developing, reshaping itself based on life experiences, rather than being fixed at birth.**
>
> berkely.edu

So, one is never too old! 'Environmental therapy' though? From my perspective this is a rather insidious and disrespectful choice of words.

If human beings of all ages were quite simply *permitted* to play, to exercise a healthy curiosity with the innate skills that they are born with, exploring all their six senses, their imagination, their own personal truth, their intuition and their physical, emotional, psychic and empathic abilities (which is what acting and spontaneous improvisation is all about), then they won't be in need of 'environmental therapy'. But, yes, if people are not permitted to play in this way, then therapy of some sort is probably the only option available to them to understand what could be wrong with them … or, put it another way, what is wrong with their environment.

Let us now take a brief look at more recent discoveries in neuroscience, regarding the unappreciated genius of the inner child that we neglect or leave behind.

> **EEG studies of the brains of children under five show that they permanently function in alpha mode – the state of altered consciousness in an adult – rather than the beta mode of ordinary mature consciousness. Children are open to far more information in The Field (The Quantum Field of Sub-Atomic Information) than the average adult.**
>
> Lynne McTaggart,
> *The Field* 2001:181

Alpha brain waves are associated with relaxed alertness, enhanced learning, creativity, peak performance, imagination, visualisation and intuition. As we grow up and enter the 'real' world we are too often encouraged to forget this rather blissful, playful state of awareness. We are persuaded to develop the beta mode of so-called 'mature' consciousness.

As we 'grow up' we are disciplined by our parents and society to understand what is right and wrong; what is the most perfect thing to aspire to or achieve. We hardly question it. How can we when we are so small? If we do, we are invariably punished. In school, goals and agendas are set for us by the government and educational departments: 'grown ups' who don't know us personally and who very often have other political or financial interests at heart. I state the obvious.

Plato once said: '*Education is teaching our children to desire the right things.*' I think he was giving an oration to a bunch of political leaders, who were trying to design the best way to control a population ... So, I ask the players in the Playground, *who* has the right to decide what the right things are?

There is no simple answer. I can only answer for myself. *I* decide. When I say 'I', I mean my inner intuitive being. My Self. The being behind and beyond the Mask.

Let me try to explain. It begins with feelings. I start with my gut feelings, my belly brain, which I have learnt to trust. I value my intuitive, gut feelings over and above my rational mind (although both are valuable in different contexts). Where do these gut feelings or inspirations come from? They come from my subconscious or subliminal awareness.

When I get these feelings, it is as if I am receiving a premonition. A part of me, an inner voice or energetic frequency is sensually informing me of something I need to give my attention to. The information arrives in subtle emotional waves and then in pictures in my mind's eye. Images. Imaginative pictures. It is a highly creative, informative and emotive experience that I have learnt not to repress when living, acting and teaching.

I believe Carl Jung was referring to precisely this, when he spoke of what he described as our *second psychic centre*.

I will be discussing this and many other mysterious faculties of the human 'mind' in the next chapter. But for now let us simply agree that we are not numbers or machines, nor should we, nor can we be assessed by computerised right brain tick-box systems.

Neuroscientists are realising things about the 'human mind' that completely contradict what we thought we knew. In a similar way to the coding of our genes, our brains are all wired in uniquely individual ways.

It is clear that the average schooling system has not been designed to cater for these unique creative and cognitive differences that we are born with. Our sensitive beings are forced by the outcomes of nonsensical statistical evidence to comply with the stressful demands of an increasingly fast moving, capitalist world, which attempts to distract us from our true creative genius and channel our uniformed biological beings into chicken coops.

As we 'grow up' into a blinkered beta consciousness, we become convinced that the right and best, safest and fittest thing to do is to be a stereotype, pigeon-holed and type cast. We are forced (force ourselves) to separate ourselves from our original child-like knowing; our slow, sensual, playful and eternally wise, intuitive being. It's like an elephant cutting its own trunk off.

Here, I take the opportunity to refer back to the concept of neuroplasticity, and the evidence that through play-acting we can not only reconnect to our original being, but stimulate the growth of new vital neural connections.

Separation

> One of the most obvious psychological roots of theatrical performance is that of PLAY. All mammals, especially advanced primates, like to explore the environment around them, exercise innate skills and test the limits of their own physical and mental capacities. The survival advantage of such an instinctual tendency is self-evident ... Because of our advanced brains we have an innate capacity for, and inclination towards, mental play, which we call fantasy ... For the adult, theatre and films are among the last socially acceptable outlets for the instinct of mental play.

> Glenn D. Wilson (d.o.b. 1942), psychologist.
> *Psychology for Performing Artists* 1994:17

We want to play. We want to connect. If we are not utterly depressed, we seek ways of making new connections all the time. When we act and improvise spontaneously together we connect physically, mentally and emotionally.

Theatre and film are indeed two of the last, imaginatively creative outlets for *adult* mental and physical play ... for some. Some play and some watch. It's an 'us and them' thing. They, the 'stars', are like silicone gods that entertain us, capturing our imaginations, while we eat popcorn on a comfortable seat in front of a screen. We think we are connected with them, but in fact we are far removed. We are disconnected.

I personally prefer to cultivate the idea that the whole of life is theatre or a film that we can actively get involved in. The experiential games I give people to play enable them to break through the screens that separate us ... from others and our Self.

When we look around us, we see something strange happening. The *separation* between 'us' and 'them' is on the increase. More and more people are communicating long distance as it were, via a cable or a screen or text messages within a virtual world that is imaginatively created for them by highly influential consumer marketing experts; a world where live or living theatre is dying a slow death in the strangle hold of financially successful block buster, 3D digital screen and on-line entertainment. We now exist in a world full of big brother cameras, where the word 'private' is taking on a whole new meaning; a world where people are becoming more and more entranced by dubious marketing tactics in a profit-orientated world; a world where only 'they', the exclusive few, actually profit. Again I state the obvious.

Despite the obvious benefits of the World Wide Web and more 'online connectedness', it seems that more and more people are becoming faces on a screen, desperate for attention, dis-contented, dis-connected, cut off, isolated, lonely, stressed, redundant, fearful beings, eating more and moving less, precisely because of the success of this advanced technological phenomenon and its power to market consumer products and toys for pornographic and violent distraction i.e. games that are not healthy for our minds, bodies, hearts or fields of consciousness. I state the absurdly obvious.

With the rapid breakdown of natural communities as we once knew them less than a hundred years ago and the creation of new on-line communities or government funded communities (big societies), people are increasingly exposed to an artificially created world and have less and less practise in open, honest and direct face-to-face, communication with one another. In parallel, we witness how modern weapons of war are all about distance and separation from the deed. Yes, I state the obvious.

Presence

Direct eye-to-eye communication is something that is highly valued in the acting dimension. We hear it said about great actors: 'That actor has presence.' Presence? What is this mysterious quality that is so hard to define? Presence is nothing more than the ability to be truly present. It is nothing less than the embodiment of a whole body sensory awareness, the ability to hold direct eye contact, to read body-language, to be engaged, centred, connected, responsive and authentically alive. It involves a heightened awareness of the non-verbal articulation of feelings, one's own and of others. Presence requires emotional intelligence and real listening skills. It is a form of sensory intelligence that is *tuned into* and *connected* with other human beings in the NOW.

Once mastered, this form of intelligence can even function over long distances, without the aid of radios, telephones or computers!

We are referring once again to an *Alpha wave* state of awareness, to an *Intuitive Intelligence*, a *heightened consciousness*; what some describe as *Extra Sensory Perception (ESP)*. Lynne McTaggart describes all this beautifully in her book *The Field* (published in 2001). She explains, for example, how extensive and comprehensive research into ESP has revealed, with staggeringly convincing scientific evidence that people, 'average' people can, with the use of their minds, influence the way both animate and inanimate objects behave. This is apparently even more so in the case of artistic people and those who are more in tune with their *unconscious, intuitive awareness* ... in particular, where there is the presence of strong bonds of love, need and connection.

> **(ESP Tests revealed) an altered view of the world. People were more likely to succeed (in ESP tests) if instead of believing in a distinction between themselves and the world, and seeing individual people and things as isolated and divisible, they viewed everything as a connected continuum of interrelations – and also if they understood that there were other ways to communicate than through the usual channels.**

McTaggart 2001:176

In the Playground, we learn about empathy, self-awareness, generosity, trust, presence, playfulness and connectivity; all qualities of accomplished actors, but which require an un-learning of some of things we learnt in school. The result is that we can breathe more deeply. We can focus better. We can improvise more confidently, spontaneously, flexibly, creatively, imaginatively and intuitively around situations that would otherwise logically have made us afraid, hide our true potential or run in the other direction.

Let us now move on to the next chapter and enter the enlightening, shadowy and paradoxical dimension of the actor.

CHAPTER FOUR

THE MIRROR

"There is no use in trying," said Alice; "one can't believe in impossible things."

"I dare say you haven't had much practice," said the Queen. "When I was your age, I always did it for half an hour a day. Why, sometimes I believed as many as six impossible things before breakfast."

Lewis Carroll 1871

WHAT I AM about to reveal are acting secrets, concepts and techniques, which I believe many more people could benefit from knowing about. Not just professional actors.

The real impact of these revelations occurs in the *experience of playing*, rather than in the reading about it, so in order to facilitate something of this experience, I will now begin to include a few case studies and examples of games, thereby leading the reader gradually towards the heart and underbelly of the Playground. There we will encounter the player's psychic *Shadow* and the phenomenon of the *Creative Observer*.

This will be immediately followed by detailed explanations and descriptions of a much larger range of games and creative challenges, with additional notes in *Chapter 5, Games: Part 1-4.*

Acting Consciously or Unconsciously

To be, or not to be: that is the question
probably the most quoted Shakespeare quote of all time.

One of the first questions I ask a group of new players is: 'So, what do you think acting is all about?' The most common answer is: 'Pretending to be someone else.'

Right from the outset, I have to gently introduce the idea that actually acting is about *being yourself,* or just *being* ... but more honestly. More truthfully. How can this be?

In order to answer this question, we need to define acting in a new way. Let us say that acting is something we all do ... not *can* do, but *do* do ... whether we are conscious of it or not. From the moment we take our first breath and open our senses to the world around us, we try to discover who we are in relation to other people and things we can touch, taste, smell, feel and see. We learn by modelling, mirroring and imitating our elders and our peers. We learn quickly from the reactions we get in response to the expression of our feelings. We learn to *act up, act out,* throw our toys out of the pram, we re-*act*, re-en*act* and dream up situations with our dolls, tractors, farm animals, building blocks, play dough and painting tools; we play, dress up and dream. Ultimately, we search for our Self in relation to the world around us.

We explore ways of *being*, we assimilate ideas and make them our own. As we grow up, we find more or less effective ways to get what we want and what we need. If we can, we persuade, influence, coerce and control. *And we all do this*. Wittingly or unwittingly we shape our world and manipulate our way through it ... for better or for worse. We respond. We are responsible. Sometimes we hide the justifications for our actions in very clever or subtle ways. Sometimes we justify our actions in extremely inventive ways. We learn to survive ... not necessarily to thrive.

So, yes, in this sense, we all act! But we don't always know how or why we do it. We develop unconscious habits. Over time, we forget how we got to being the character or 'personality' we now are and we end up thinking that this is who we really are. In part this is true. We are complex. We have different faces for different situations. Is the person that we see in the mirror on a Monday morning the same as the person that goes out on a Friday night? This personality or person we are now, which we either want to be or don't want to be, with all its facets, has been rehearsed and developed to perfection all our lives. It has got us to where we are now, safely or relatively safely, but mostly intact. This being, these ways of being, are therefore also, in the majority of cases, our defences, our protections, our projections, our cover ups, our back-ups, our comfort or safety zones.

We develop an outer shell, a Mask (or Masks) to protect a very soft, vulnerable centre; a core that might not want to be exposed or hurt.

Learning to act consciously i.e. taking one's innate acting skills to *new* levels of awareness, has the potential of reversing this process. The outer shell becomes much more transparent, flexible and inter-changeable, mercurial even, while the central core of one's being becomes powerful and strong, capable of almost anything, with an upright spine and a steady balance.

Having played with literally hundreds of different players, and additionally having shared my observations and experiences with many other people from different walks of life in different languages, I have come to the conclusion that the vast majority know, I mean *really know deep down inside*, that they are not manifesting, living or being all that they can be or want to be.

We become someone, who in totality we are not, in response to social pressures.

Clive Barker 1977:213

WOLFGANG, 30 YEARS OLD, GERMAN: Wolfgang was a tall, rather lugubrious, big boned character with large, sensitive eyes. He attended my play sessions in West Berlin in the 1980's, before the Berlin Wall came down. Initially, he was very quiet, serious and on first appearance rather typically Germanic, 'correct' and academic. He was studying to become a lawyer.

There was something sad about him that I couldn't quite work out. I had no idea what brought him to Playground, until one day he told me that his father had insisted that he follow a career in Law. His heart was not in it. His dream was to audition for the Strasberg Actors Studio in New York, but his father would be furious if he ever found out that he was attending acting classes! I have to admit I was surprised, because until that point I had had no indication that Wolfgang's aim was to be a professional actor. He seemed to enjoy the games, but he was holding something back.

I set about challenging him with some *method acting* games that draw *truth* and *authenticity* out of a player ... *method* being an acting technique that evolved in America, in particular explored by the Strasberg School of Acting (see *Opposing Truths – Games Part 3/Authenticity*). Wolfgang responded with such conviction and emotion it was almost painful to watch. But that was just the beginning. From that moment on he became stronger and more centred. He began to come out of his shell and revealed a very different personality, a passion and an enormous creative talent. I coached him in some audition pieces and encouraged him to book a flight to New York, where he attended an audition. He was granted a place at the Studio.

I do not know how Wolfgang fared later in life, whether he made it as a professional actor or not, but I am certain that his experience of 'coming out' as an actor will have greatly enhanced his performance in any subsequent activity or career choice in life, not least as a Lawyer!

What I have encountered again and again in the Playground, and it fascinates me, is that beneath the exterior of who we present ourselves to be, there is invariably a *whole other world*, sometimes the complete opposite of what is being presented on the outside.

Wolfgang chose to hold onto his dream and, despite his fears, pursued it. Usually the reverse happens. Many find it easier and safer to ignore what is really going on inside. We suppress the unwanted within ourselves, because at some point we have learnt that it is undesirable. This is exactly how the *Shadow* operates. I will be speaking much more about this later.

Few people naturally integrate the inner and the outer world. Those who do are extraordinary and we sense that. There is an integrity, a charisma, an aura about them that is arresting. Tom Hardy is an actor that radiates this form of self-assurance and confidence. He is clearly a powerful player, who is not afraid of being dangerous. Some might not like him or agree, but I respect the way he managed to transform his life and his commitment to authenticity both on screen and off.

The opposite extreme might present itself in a person who is terrified that someone will discover their inner world or discover that they are not really who they say they are, that they are a fraud; like a tiny rabbit caught in headlights, rigid with the fear of being deemed abnormal or unsuccessful or even not integral in the eyes of others. This is not *being*. This is *not* being.

This type of fearful response can be triggered simply by someone becoming more intimate with us ... getting closer to the part of us that is not supposed to be seen or exist. We are talking about a chronic *fear of failure* that is far worse than we allow ourselves to believe ... a fear of not being accepted in the 'real world' as we really are.

Stage Fright

The most potent weapon in the hands of the oppressor is the mind of the oppressed
Stephen Bantu Biko, founder of the Black Consciousness Movement

Most of the players that come to the Playground are 'normal' people with regular jobs and regular lives. The majority arrive with a real concern or fear of performing in front of other people. Some of them are literally shaking.

SAMANTHA, 38 YEARS OLD, ENGLISH: On the surface, to most people, Samantha was a 'normal' human being who worked in a supermarket. She came to my classes in 2003. Sam seemed quiet, reserved, somehow locked away in her own world, worrying about what she looked like, meticulously painting her already beautiful face, shaping her eye-brows and stroking her hair into place. When others were not present, alone with me in a room, she persistently insisted, in a whispered voice: 'I'm not really like this you know.' I always assured her that I knew that was true.

But still, on being invited to play games with the group, she froze rigid and couldn't breathe properly. She stood terrified or watched from the wings. It took a long time for her to relax enough to join in. She really wanted to, but just couldn't. Instead of immersing herself in creative imagination, as a child would in play, she was constantly worried about what other people were thinking of her, that they would judge her wrongly and think her ideas were weird.

Gradually it was revealed that Sam had, in fact, been subjected to a kind of brainwashing from the age of ten (for the sake of confidentiality I have been asked not to go into the details) and, as a result, locked herself away in her room for most of her youth with only a T.V. set for company. She did not play at all as a teenager should. Sam was encouraged to admit herself into a mental hospital at 19 for help, but that experience, along with the stigma and medications involved, only further messed with her mind.

After several months of encouraging Sam to play (yes, it took a while, but she loved the Playground and kept returning, gradually joining in more and more) her real Self began to emerge. She was able to show us that she is, in fact, an extra-ordinarily intelligent and highly articulate being, with a vibrant and prolific imagination, who can speak in many accents with ease. She transformed into a uniquely funny comedienne, with a very quick wit and a beautiful soft, warm smile. I can assure you that Sam is now living life so much more to the full, has married one of the other players and dresses up in crazy, glamorous outfits, laughing and joking. She is currently writing a book about her life.

When Samantha came to me, she was afraid not only of exposing who she really was or wanted to be for fear of rejection, but was deeply concerned that she would not be seen as anything *but* the Mask that she had created for herself … that she would never be seen as the being she felt and knew she really was inside.

The case that I have just described is extreme, but to a greater or lesser degree typical of many who suffer from stage fright. Stage fright is good, when we are talking about an adrenaline rush and 'butterflies in the stomach'. It helps us focus. But nerves arising from the wrong form of self-consciousness or self-analysis can become crippling if one suffers from a *fear of failure in the eyes of others*. It is then impossible to immerse oneself in the joy and passion of playful acting.

In such cases, I find that surreal madness and absurdity offer a brilliant release from the expectations, pressures and stresses of a prescribed and judged 'normality'. The crazy acting games that I have developed for adults to play, scramble and dis-connect (switch off) the analytical part of the brain and thereby reduce addictions to external judgement. This release has a fantastically positive impact on the player's ability to love, laugh, relax and enjoy themselves again. It gives them a growing sense of acceptance, plus a safety zone where they can *focus on what they really want and dream of in life*.

In the Playground, debilitating forms of stage fright rapidly become a thing of the past. In its place arrives *clarity of focus, self-respect* and a *deeper respect and compassion for others*. These qualities are essential if the players are to learn some of the more advanced acting techniques that I describe later.

The Secrets of Body Language

> I once had a close rapport with a teenager who seemed 'mad' when she was with other people, but relatively normal when she was with me. I treated her rather as I would a Mask ... that is to say, I was gentle, and didn't impose my reality on her. One thing that amazed me was her perceptiveness about other people – it was as if she was a body language expert.
>
> Keith Johnstone (d.o.b. 1933), pioneer of improvisational theatre.
> *IMPRO* 1981:15

We don't observe people much in the real world directly or openly, because it's rude to stare. Staring at other people is interpreted as threatening or menacing, an attempt at seduction or even stupid, child-like naivety. So, we end up spying on each other secretly. We comment on what we notice behind people's backs.

In the acting dimension, conscious, prolonged and deep observation of oneself and others in action is indispensable. Open, honest discussions about what we have observed are integral to the process of discovery. Without these observations one could not begin to understand human behaviour, intelligently read or interpret the signs of body-language.

For those that don't know what *reading body language* is, it is the ability to tune into non-verbal signs and signals; to sense the unspoken, behind the words people speak. The signals that one might pick up include physical qualities, facial expressions, eye movements, the tone of voice, breathe, gestures, physical attitudes and stances. The skills required include the acknowledgement of feelings, an understanding of *sub-text* (i.e. what we're thinking, but not saying) and an appreciation of *authenticity* (for both Subtext and Authenticity see *Chapter 5: Games, Part 3/Transformation and Truth*).

All this requires the use of *direct eye-contact, empathic listening, stillness, awareness of breathe, space and timing*. Really these skills cannot be described fully or learnt from a book. They have to be witnessed, recognised, felt and shared in an experiential and safe setting, precisely because we are talking about *feelings*.

But now here comes the interesting bit. My experience of teaching people the intricacies of body-language in the Playground has shown me that we can all read body language, much better than we think we can or admit openly. Often we don't register the signs *consciously*; it is in retrospect that we realise that we actually picked up on the signals!

Maybe we just don't trust our abilities to know, to show, to act on or *own* what we really sense and feel, but the truth is, possibly with the exception of rare individuals* (see footnote about *Autism and Asperger*), we all get hunches and gut feelings.

There appears to be a sort of silent agreement that we shouldn't speak about what we intuitively feel is going on or a built in understanding that feelings aren't relevant in our understanding of the world around us. In the 'real world' we are taught to uphold certain codes of behaviour. We learn, in the 'real world' that it could be stupid, disadvantageous, existentially threatening or even fatal *to act on what we really know deep inside*. It could be fatal *not* to, too.

RACHAEL, 40 YEARS OLD, ENGLISH: Rachael was tall, beautiful, intelligent, but slightly slouched in posture. She had large breasts and tended to hide them by rounding her upper back and shoulders. She had beautiful eyes, but didn't let you see them. She seemed to be trying to disappear both physically and vocally. She was nervous about performing, that is until she experienced the confidence games (*Chapter 5, Games: Part 3, Confidence*). In those revelatory sessions about body-language, she learnt rapidly how playing high status can transform not only how you feel, but the way other people relate to you and treat you. So much so that the next time she visited her uncle, she sat bravely opposite him, for the first time in her life with a straight back, looked him directly in the eyes and said: 'I remember what you did to me when I was a little girl.' She described this moment as being immensely empowering and a major break-through for herself as a person.

*AUTISM and ASPERGER are described as 'developmental disabilities' that affect the way a person communicates and how they experience the world around them. The diagnosed are described as not being able to respond normally to accepted codes of behaviour. Some don't seem to recognise emotions. Interestingly though, scientists now seem to be suggesting that we are all advantaged or disadvantaged by Autistic and Asperger 'communication disorders' to some degree or other on a continuum. And on that continuum, it seems obvious to me, we all see and feel and know things in ways that others might be completely blind to. What seems 'normal' for one is incomprehensible to another. We are all wired differently.

I propose that developing acting skills might help bridge some of the gaps of incomprehension. In this light, I would like to introduce Kaela.

KAELA 32 YEARS OLD, BRITISH: Kaela came to my classes to explore 'being', primarily as an actress, but also simply as a human-being. Both. She told me that she has been through difficult phases in her life, sometimes anxious and frustrated/dissociated, not knowing what she wanted from life or what life wanted from her.

Kaela enjoys very much working with horses and primates (studying ape conversation) and has explored being a stunt woman. She dances and sings beautifully, is naturally musical, with the ability to pick up any instrument and learn it quickly. She can memorise and retain large amounts of text easily and quickly. She is highly intelligent and curious, endlessly pursuing studies in maths/ theoretical physics and neuroscience/psychology among many other tangents. She writes exquisite poetry and prose ... although much or all of this she would deny. She is now studying method acting in London. Kaela was officially diagnosed as 'autistic (HFA/Asperger)' in 2012.

I asked her if she could write a bit about her experience of autism, also in relation to the experience of 'learning to act'. She wrote 2-3 pages of captivatingly convincing polemics, which unfortunately I have had to trim down to their bare essentials for this book:

> *'I find it vexing, attempting to commit to any description or understanding of what it means to be on the autistic spectrum …This is partly because, like anything, it is so variable between individuals, but also because I personally have a pathological intolerance of the illusory man made boundaries and definitions that plague our existence!*
>
> *Whereas reality is an infinite boundary-less interchange of energy, everything in our interpretative human pseudo-reality is filtered through intricately compartmentalised expectations, conditioned through society and perversely rigid cultures. This is so inescapably powerful that some-times a label or 'loophole' of sorts like autism can become a lifeline simply in order to access a level of openness and acceptance or purity of perception that, if we operated on a level of direct truth as other species do, we should be accessing automatically anyway.*
>
> *… it is strange that 'acting' is the only capacity in our human world where we can accept all manner of dramatic and intensely real behaviours from people, allowing this to deeply affect us, yet not proceed to define those people forever more by the behaviour we witnessed from them! (– because it was 'pretend'/only a 'story'!!). – So acting is another one of those 'loopholes' allowing we poor decrepit humans to – in the words of Stella Adler – 'Be whatever you are up there' ... and wildly explore the boundless wonders of our existence, sculpting our own true transformative stories as we should be doing anyway.*
>
> *In the case of autism, experiences are majorly intensified, the nature of which experiences varying between individuals, but the overall effect is that some simple scenarios can disproportionately become neurologically over-whelming, inhibiting behavioural functioning and potentially leading to meltdown or shutdown. The nature of the open ended rigorous pursuit of*

honing our artistry as actors is a perfect management system for an intensified neurology! And it is precisely the essential antidote to the harmful inhibitive effects of society, hence is mostly a process of undoing conditioning and removing false psychological constructs; learning to 'get out the way' of our true being and creativity, to release and express our internal experiences. Other animals know how to do this instinctively, hence they are so captivating – and also many people on the autistic spectrum feel an especially intense affinity with them, and a level of intimacy that would cause excruciating discomfort or even physical pain with other fellow humans. People in real acting environments are significantly stripped down closer to our animal selves and so largely the 'symptoms' of autism can essentially disappear. And so this 'acting' is really something that should form a central part of our education and lifestyle in a healthy culture, and would hugely benefit those on the spectrum; both directly/symptomatically and also by aiding in neutralising the inhibitive stigmatic perception from society that is so disabling.'

De-Mechanisation

How can emotions, the language of the heart and the soul, 'freely' manifest themselves throughout a person's body, if that very instrument is 'mechanised', automated in its muscle structures and insensible to 90% of its possibilities?

Augustus Boal, 1931-2009,
founder of Theatre of the Oppressed, 1992:40

Learning to act skilfully requires that we rediscover suppressed parts of ourselves. This means we have to break habits. We have to *de-mechanise* our bodies and minds in order to free up, get into touch with and release our emotions and feelings.

There are many reasons why we hide or ignore parts of ourselves, why we choose not to act on what we intuitively know, hear, feel and see, why we separate ourselves from others or even from our real core self.

Tunnel vision is undoubtedly one of them. We are all perfectly capable of seeing things with 'blinkers' on. We are human and this appears to be an inbuilt human skill that we all have. We zoom in on a part of the picture and lose sight of the whole picture. This ability means that we are perfectly capable of developing blind spots, things we simply don't *want* to see or *choose* not to see about ourselves and others. Strangely enough, in retrospect, and seen from a different perspective we very often say that we knew those things all the time!

Humans are wonderfully complex and at times extraordinarily evasive, not just out of respect, ignorance or fear of society's established moral codes of behaviour, nor because we blindly fall in love or choose to mistrust or ignore our own intuition. Sometimes we become deluded because of a deplorable lack of really interesting creative challenges that speak to our heart. We shut down, resign and accept second best. We cope.

And then there's force of habit. I am not talking about 'addiction'. That is a subject that I am not qualified to discuss in depth ... although I do think perhaps that we are all addicted to something or other. Sugar. T.V. Sex. Caffeine. Fast cars. Dogs. Cats. Work. Sport. External appearances. Neuroses. Dogmas. Religion.

We stick to beliefs and habits, adhere to rituals and social conventions for the sake of pleasure, survival, safety and group acceptance ... sometimes out of pure laziness, comfort and convenience too! We avoid the stress and complications of change or of challenging conventions. We choose to be blind to things we don't want to think about, because it's easier. We seek distraction from what we really feel inside. We stop questioning the appropriateness of some of the things we do automatically in our daily lives, saying: 'Hi. How are you?' without having the time to or even wanting to know. Eating lunch, because the clock says 'it's lunchtime'. Shopping, because we're bored. Saying we like things, when we don't. Saying we're fine, when we aren't. Celebrating Christmas, just because everyone else is, with false snow, money we don't have and gifts we don't want. And the majority don't even believe in Father Christmas, let alone God. What is more real ... theatre or reality? We allow ourselves to become comfortably dumb. We become *mechanised*.

The superb thing about learning acting is that it throws an unconventional light on a whole range of ways in which *we censor 90% of our cognitive, emotional and sensory faculties.*

The de-mechanisation games that I describe later in *Games, Part 2 and 3 e.g. Daily Repetitions, Words Cushions* (which usually ends up as a cushion fight) and *Abstract Madness*, are all designed specifically and initially to disorientate and scramble the players' brains in a chaotically funny way. Without worrying what they look like or what a fool they are being, the players end up doing mad and irrational things that they never thought they would or could do. Not surprisingly, they love it. It gets them out of the rut of a depressing existence. The games break down normal habits of response and behaviour without conflict. They *de-mechanise* physical and mental patterns, freeing the player up to literally leap-frog over any fear of change. This type of crazy game is designed to awaken hidden psychic abilities in preparation for the more advanced acting techniques that come later.

Here is a taster of one of the de-mechanisation games I have invented. In *Games, Part 1: The Approach* and *Games, Part 2: Imagination,* you will find other and similar de-mechanisation games, both simple and advanced.

ABSURD HABITS: You need a park-bench (made out of three chairs in a line) in the middle of the stage area. Two players (A + B) sit on the park-bench and have a conversation about anything. It could be a polite conversation about the ducks; the weather; the clothes they are wearing; the shopping they've just bought; their general heath; the last film they saw … whatever. BUT, *before* the improvisation commences the two players will have both secretly been given a peculiar habit that is triggered by something the other player says or does. Here are some examples:

> A has been secretly told that every time B says the word 'I' or 'You', A has a panic attack.

> B has been secretly told that every time A touches his/her hair, head or face, B declares passionate love to A.

> OR

> A has secretly been told that every time B smiles or laughs, A giggles like crazy.

> B has secretly been told that every time A shifts their feet, B acts as if A has just farted.

> OR

> A has secretly been told that every time B says 'Yes', A breaks out into song.

> B has secretly been told that every time A breaks into song, B has to block his/her ears and hide under the park bench.

I hope the reader can imagine the impact that these triggers and habits make and can see how, if you set them up right, the one habit or trigger will feed or set off the other.

Note: Sometimes, the two players who are improvising cotton on to what the other player's trigger is e.g. A might pick up on the fact that whenever they touch their hair, face or head ... B declares passionate love. A could then decide to constantly touch their hair, in which case B would have to constantly declare passionate love. In this way they can have fun manipulating each other's behaviour!

The Power of the Eyes

For beautiful eyes, look for the good in others.

Audrey Hepburn

The eyes! One of the actor's most powerful assets and tools for communicative play. Are we taught about these secrets in school? No.

Being able to maintain direct and prolonged eye contact in acting is essential. In 'real life' we shy away from this, understandably, but when you watch top film and stage actors you will notice that they are very good at holding eye-contact for long periods of time. They are very conscious of the use and impact of their eyes.

What are these things called eyes? We see with them. When we close them, our other senses become alert to hearing, sensing, touch, taste and feeling. Eyes can see invisible things too ... invisible to some and visible to others. We see what we want to see ... or what we are told to see. We dream and imagine constantly. Some say that 'Eyes are doors to the Soul'. I experience them as being 'Windows of the Heart'. Eyes, or the lowering of the eyelids, tell a whole story about what is going on inside ... or not. Evasiveness is most common nowadays, which maybe in part accounts for the popular use of sun glasses.

The majority know the power of the eyes to reveal the truth. 'Look me in the eyes.' People can hypnotise, mesmerize, command and control others with their eyes (that is, if they are blessed with sight). The armed forces, police, politicians and some civil servants are clearly advised or trained to use very direct eye contact in certain situations, for example, when they are interviewing or arrest-ing people. Yes, eyes can 'arrest' attention.

What many don't know, though, is that through a different focusing of the eyes one can reach other states of awareness or consciousness. In acting we learn about this. For example, panoramic or peripheral vision gives a heightened *intuitive* awareness. Carlos Castaneda tells us something of this in his book *Don Juan*, and in NLP we learn about the movements of eyes ... how to read the movements of the eyes in general.

I'll be writing more about the eyes, from the perspective of an actor in *Games, Part 4*, when I describe the Confidence Games. But really it is impossible to describe the various eye techniques actors can use, or indeed the power of the eyes, in words. I leave that to Shakespeare. In the Playground the power of the eyes has to be seen and felt. I merely touch on this here, because it is the eyes that see through the Mask.

> Thou tell'st me there is murder in mine eye:
> 'Tis pretty, sure, and very probable,
> That eyes, that are the frail'st and softest things,
> Who shut their coward gates on atomies,
> Should be call'd tyrants, butchers, murderers!
> Now I do frown on thee with all my heart;
> And, if mine eyes can wound, now let them kill thee;
> Now counterfeit to swound; why now fall down;
> Or, if thou canst not, O! for shame,
> Lie not, to say mine eyes are murderers.

Shakespeare, Scene V, Act III, Phoebe *As You Like It*

The Power of the Mask

Humans love to make-believe. We love to pretend to be. The phenomenon of the MASK ... the external face of who we are ... is a vast, deep and potentially dangerous subject. I will speak more about the potential dangers in relation to *hypnosis* and *trance states* later. But let's start with what is commonly known about the Mask; that is, the obvious – what the majority of life's players are familiar with.

Clearly depicted in the theatrical symbol of the two faces of tragedy and comedy, the Mask is a theatrical device used to assume a different personality, like the red nose of a clown (the smallest mask in the world!), the hooked nose of a witch or the half masks of Comedia dell'arte. At 'masked balls' the Mask may be used as a fashion statement, or to represent an archetype, a building, the spirit of an animal, a flower, a monster or a dead icon. In sports arenas we see the uniform identity of a national flag painted all over everyone's faces. At political rallies the mask may be used to represent some political figure, a popular idol or a collective idea, like the revolutionary Guy Fawkes *vox populi* Mask from the film *V for Vendetta*. In crime and warfare, masks are used as a means of camouflaging or hiding who one really is. Sunglasses are a type of mask too. The mafia, rock stars and, of course, the common player, like Sam Brown, use them to glamorise, mystify their image or hide their eyes. Dark glasses nowadays are one of the most globally accepted, commonly used and valued Masks for personal transformation.

I continue to state the obvious. There are strange taboos and stigmas attached to the concept of the Mask, some of which are utterly ridiculous, perverse even. If we attend a party where everyone is invited to come in costume, then the majority will have no problem dressing up in all sorts of fantastical ways ... but, in everyday life?

Certain cultures and societies marginalise and brutally ostracise men and women who paint their faces with make-up, labelling them gays or whores. A man may feel compelled by his religion to grow a beard and have long hair. In other cultures or eras they would be persecuted for the same. In some cultures a woman's face has to be covered almost completely. In other cultures and in certain contexts it has become perfectly acceptable, expected even, for women to wear make-up *all the time*, even false eye-lashes in bed, or to literally have the whole face surgically lifted or dyed orange. If it's not tragic, it's comic. What is unacceptable for one, for example tattoos and piercings, is a mark of beauty for another.

What is less obvious is that amidst all the cultural 'dos and don'ts' of masks and pretences, many people don't realise that their natural daily facial expression, with or without make-up, is a type of Mask too.

The truth is that we learn to hold characteristic expressions as a way of maintaining our personalities, and we're far more influenced by faces than we realise.
Keith Johnstone 1981:150

There are hundreds of individual muscles in the face. Meditation, happiness and love can have a rejuvenating effect on those muscles. We know this. Some facial contractions are genetically inherited, but we know that environmental, cultural and educational factors play a dominant role in the way we orientate our external Mask to the world around us. We put on a brave face to hide layers of unspoken fear, confusion, silenced anger or disillusionment about life. The Mask assumes a delightful smile, a cheesy grin, a stiff upper lip, a clenched jaw or a permanent scowl, a frown that is etched into the brow. As we grow older unconscious habits form, for example, gritting one's teeth and bearing it, smiling constantly in a willingness to please, pursing the lips in martyred resignation, holding back a cry of anger or truth in a tight jaw or a closed aching throat ...all these can become permanent facial expressions, which actually reveal much about what's going on *behind* the Mask.

URSULA, 24 YEARS OLD, GERMAN: Ursula was a fun, outgoing, boyish girl. She came to me to gain more confidence in improvisation. She was a versatile and flexible player in many ways, with one strange exception. She found it very hard to be angry. She smiled and laughed nearly all the time. I began to notice that her jaw was very tense, despite her good humour, as if she was holding on to something that she wasn't saying.

One day I suggested she play the role of someone who was *very* angry. She remained vigilantly resistant to going there, despite her own wish to immerse herself in the role. Finally, I introduced a creative challenge called *Sense Memory*. This is an acting technique that I explain later in this chapter and again in much more depth in the *Underbelly Games Section, Part 5*. It is a vital technique that takes the players to the heart of what's going on inside. As a result of the challenge, Ursula burst into tears and shouted angrily: '*Ich will nicht immer glücklich sein!!!*' (I don't always want to be happy!) This encounter with her real inner feelings enabled her to unveil to us that she had been adopted by foster parents when she was five years old. Her adoptive parents were really wonderful people, and had always been very concerned that she was happy. She never permitted herself, out of respect for their feelings, to show that she was sad or troubled. Hence the tense jaw and the Mask of happiness.

FIXED FACIAL EXPRESSIONS: A drama game I invented, which demonstrates the absurdity of holding facial muscles in permanently tense positions. As banal as it appears to be, it does in fact demonstrate the undeniable two way relationship between body and mind. *Our physical state of tension affects our psyche, just as our psychic state affects our physical being.*

Two players sit on the park bench (as before). I ask one player to assume a fixed facial expression of anger and I ask the other player to assume a fixed facial expression of happiness. I ask them to hold these facial expressions no matter what happens! I invite them to have a conversation about anything that comes to mind e.g. hobbies, holidays, work, politics, films, pets, food. What invariably happens is that the Mask takes over ... totally affecting the player's character, voice, emotion, reactions and invariably also the things they choose to talk about e.g.

> The Angry Masks says: What the fuck are you smiling at???!!!!
> The Happy Mask says: It's my Birthday today!!!
> Angry: So, you invited me here, because you thought I'd give you a present?!
> Happy: No. I just love you. You're my best friend.
> Angry: Fuck off.
> Happy: You're so funny!!
> ... and so on and so forth.

This can be played with various combinations of fixed facial expressions: Sad. Petrified. Morose. Sweet. Snooty. Nosey. Lustful. The improvisations should be quite short, because it is exhausting holding the face in a tense Mask for too long.

But point made. The external mask affects the internal attitude/feelings and vice versa. There is a mind/body interaction.

Sometimes I invite the players to play with self-created Masks that they design at home and bring to the following session. The invention usually takes the players to the outer expression of the darker, archetypical, beautiful, hidden, unspoken parts of the Self within.

GERRY, 45 YEARS OLD, BRITISH: Gerry was a jokey, blokey, intellectual wit. A bit of a clown. He created an extraordinary Mask. It was an image cut out of a newspaper of a boxer's face beaten up, cut up, sweaty, bloody and swollen. It happened to be life size in the newspaper, so it fitted his face perfectly. He poked crude holes in the eyes, so he could see through the Mask and he attached rubber bands on the sides that hooked around his ears. The effect was surreal and disturbing.

Other times, I might encourage the players to design new outfits, 'looks' or complete image transformations.

MICHELLE, 54 YEARS OLD, BRITISH: Michelle, in her own words *'suffers much'*, having endured *'a myriad of abuse in her early years, neglect and abandonment'*. When she came to my play sessions, I noticed that she had no real sense of her own boundaries. She had a great ability to empathise with others though. She picked up on other people's feelings very quickly, but seemed to make them her own *'on top of her own feelings'*. She was a self-absorbed being with a heightened intuitive awareness. Hence, she had real difficulties focusing. Her thoughts were distracted, due to *'mind overwhelm'* and her eyes were constantly moving. She wore clothes that made her look like a little girl, but with greying hair there was an obvious incongruence about her appearance.

It was clear to me that her core being ... her sense of who she *really* is, her sense of self-worth... needed to be developed. So, I decided to invite her to do two different things. The first was to see a portrait of herself in her mind's eye (*Stepping into the Picture* is described in *Games, Part 4: Transformation*). In the picture, she saw a strong woman, dressed in bright shiny blue, who was in charge of a space ship. A bit of a revelation for her and all of us. Later in the same session, I invited her to play the role of an aggressive punk with spikes all over her body, which she thoroughly enjoyed.

The following session she arrived in a streamline black outfit, with her hair dyed black and tied back off her face. Her eyes were darkened with eyeliner. She looked stunning. A real transformation. Ever since then she has got stronger and stronger, more focused and astutely observant about what is going on around her in a more grounded, earthed and detached way. The space commander emerged. By that I mean that she began to make more conscious decisions about how to move, be, own and utilise the space around her. She began to create her own boundaries.

Truth & Transformation

> **I knew who I was this morning, but I've changed a few times since then.**
>
> Lewis Carroll, 1871

Experimenting with one's external appearance can be a provocative and creative force. People do this in order to make a statement about who they are or would like to be seen as being. Skilled actors do this. They experiment with external transformation, in order to step into the character they are playing. Like putting on another pair of shoes. Or a hat or coat. It's an obvious trick. What we wear makes a vast difference to the way we feel about ourselves and the way others may see us.

But, what many people don't know (this is one of those professional secrets) is that the actor's primary aim is to understand, identify with and embrace their character's internal motivation, the inner thoughts of a being i.e. *what's going on behind the Mask*.

This type of *internal* transformation requires a much deeper and more honest searching for one's own inner truth. It takes guts.

> **... the decisive factor in this process is the actor's technique of psychic penetration. The important thing is to use the role as a trampoline, an instrument with which to study what is hidden behind our everyday mask – the innermost core of our personality – in order to sacrifice it, expose it.**
>
> Jerzy Grotowski, 1933-99, Polish theatre director and theorist 1968:37

In a *Telegraph* article called *'Learning to Play'*, Miranda Sawyer interviewed Mark Rylance, then the Director and lead actor at the Globe Theatre in London, about his early years of acting training at the Royal Academy of Dramatic Art. He said: *'I learnt life skills at RADA. They tried to help me STOP acting ... I remember Hugh Crutwell loving truth and what you are yourself.'*

Mark Rylance is, in my opinion, one of the greatest actors living today. I wrote this before he was awarded an Oscar in 2016! He is capable of playing a very broad range of contrasting characters with equal conviction. I found myself completely mesmerised by his performance in the awarding winning stage production *Jerusalem*, where he played the role of hell raiser Johnny 'Rooster' Byron ... *'a performance so charismatic, so mercurial, so complete and compelling that it doesn't look like acting'* (*Evening Standard*).

How does an actor do this? How can an actor make this temporary transformation so completely and convincing that it appears as if s/he isn't acting? And even more fascinating ... how can we speak of this as 'truth'?

The answer is that the actor discovers, tunes into, uncovers and reveals a part of him/herself that one doesn't normally see. And the truth is that *we all have the potential of all parts within us somewhere.*

One might want to disagree with this or deny it, but maybe we haven't yet been in a situation extreme enough to force us to confront the reality of our deeper potential. Does anyone really know how one would behave in extreme isolation or in a situation like a Nazi concentration camp? Or if one unexpectedly became a millionaire or suddenly lost a child?

In our everyday lives we more or less unconsciously bring a required part forward in order to meet a friend, a boss, a family member or an observer. We adapt to the situation. With one person we may be relaxed and feel more like our 'normal' self. In another context we may be on guard, angry and defensive, in which case we may appear to be a completely different person. The one character is sympathetic and likeable. The other appears uptight or threatening.

Skilled actors know that it is our inner motivations (and how they play out in relationship with the people around us) that define our behaviour and our 'persona'.

By employing various techniques that involve *sense memory, imagination, empathy, subtext, awareness of body-language and status,* plus a range of other more complex techniques involving decisions about *the way we choose to see things* (all of which will be described later) the actor learns to take risks; to expose him/herself; to allow parts, or at least the potential of those parts, to come out into the open, into the light, to the forefront of his/her being. The greatest actors are not afraid of being dangerous.

Being Dangerous

> ... actors today think that being true is being nice, or being some other "set" thing. That is not the truth. That is your miserable habit of boring everybody to death.
>
> Stella Adler

Creating dramatic, truthful, interesting, inspiring and engaging characters and dramas means that the actor is invariably asked to look at and express all of those things that people don't normally want to engage with in everyday life. Sometimes actors are required to be mean, dirty and dangerous.

All humans have at least two faces. Accomplished acting and quality drama cannot be about the representation of only one aspect of one's being. A person may appear ever so 'nice' on the surface, but be secretly motivated in a completely different way. An actor has to be prepared to resonate with and embody the complete picture of a human-being and the character they are playing and they have to do it truthfully in order to be convincing.

> **With any part you play, there is a certain amount of yourself in it. There has to be, otherwise it's just not acting. It's lying.**
>
> Johnny Depp

Skilled actors dare to take risks. Taking risks means not being afraid of exposing your vulnerable self or revealing your deepest darkest imagination. It's about being at ease with this type of exposure.

The actor is able to look within and without, with both comic and tragic eyes at the very real things that motivate people (and themselves!) to hate, slander, procrastinate, trick, cheat or lie, to be weak, jealous, arrogant, hypocritical, vain, ignorant or just plain lazy, decadent, indulgent, revolting, self-centred and mean. What fun??!!! We don't have to pretend we are nice anymore! Believe it or not, this is the joyous, rich and often hysterically funny aspect of learning to act.

Let me introduce you to a rather surreal game that invites players to explore their inner psyche and invent imaginary characters that they intuitively connect with.

PRECIOUS OBJECTS: I give the players a whole bunch of symbolic and/or mundane objects to choose from. Simple things like a potato, a doll, a knife, a pair of sunglasses, a box, a bottle, a stick, a rope etc. After each has chosen an object, I help them, via a series of questions to develop a character with a name and detailed history based on their relationship with the object of their choice. I then invite two of the players to improvise a scene together in the character they have developed and in a given surreal setting. I usually give the players the setting without knowing anything about the characters they have developed for themselves. The random elements add to the suspense of the improvisation. This following scenario is typical of what can manifest:

> **Player A (male) chose a potato. Player B (also male) chose a rag doll. I told them that they were on a cliff edge in the middle of the night ... the edge of the cliff being the front edge of the stage area.**

Player B (a 40 year old solicitor's clerk, British) was sitting on the cliff edge, facing the audience and clutching his doll, looking quite sad. Player A (a 46 year old French poet) entered and walked quite fast from the back of the stage area forward towards the cliff edge. He had his eyes closed and was clutching his potato. Player B cried "STOP!!!!!!!" just in time to save A from walking over the cliff edge. A, who abruptly froze in his tracks, still with his eyes closed, asked who had cried 'stop'. A conversation ensued, where the players inventively tried to discover more about each other, who they were and why they were there etc. Player A revealed that he was blind and that his potato was his intuitive mind that always guided him. Player B revealed that the rag doll was the only love he had left in his life. It seemed that they really understood each other. A beautiful relationship evolved with both of them now perched on the edge of the cliff looking out towards the sea view (and the audience). Suddenly, A spontaneously asked B if he could hold the doll. B, rather warily, said that he could, but that he must be very careful with it and give it back. B promised he would. B gave A the doll ... but then A, without any hesitation, simply chucked the doll over the cliff edge!!! He then proceeded to do what he originally intended to do – to walk over the cliff edge. It was a shocking, but strangely funny moment that had Player B and the audience gasping for breath. Not 'nice', but great drama.

A discussion took place afterwards. Why on earth had A done that, when B had just saved his life? That wasn't very nice! Player A said that his potato had told him to help character B stop being so clingy and narrow-minded ... to 'let go' of attachment.

Acting enables us to reach deep inside, to respond authentically in the moment and to test the impact of treading over perceived moral boundaries. It enables us to take the risk of doing what humans do, but more *truthfully, courageously and openly*, in a way that elevates humanity out of a mechanised normality into a more conscious zone. It is about exposing all aspects of human nature.

Herein lies real danger. Where are the boundaries? Where are the limits? Where is the edge? Is it safe? How far can one immerse oneself in the role, the feelings without endangering other players? How can one be dangerous and safe at the same time? Is it possible to go over the top in any direction, to go right over the cliff edge into the unknown, the forbidden and the unacceptable? Of course not! So, at what point does an actor decide to stop? And to stop what ... if everything is essentially human?

In the profession this is controversial issue, which could be reduced down to matter of artistic or moral taste. Clearly, there have to be strict rules and conventions that uphold the sanctity of the theatrical 'temple', just as there are rules and laws in life that prevent accidents and safe guard human rights and lives. This is good. But if theatre is to be a real mirror of society and throw a light on the shadows of what goes on behind closed doors, where are the boundaries? Are there any boundaries?

Yes. In fact, there are such strong artistic censoring mechanisms in place and well tested elitist reservations about what one is permitted to do on stage ... about what is classified as 'good acting' ... so much so that many experienced practitioners wouldn't dream of 'pushing the envelope' or exposing themselves too much. Some practitioners are very tentative about engaging in, what they describe as *psycho drama* in a theatrical context, as it could be considered to be voyeuristic 'masturbation'. And I agree, to a degree.

Powerful acting is like dancing on a knife edge, where one has to be vigilant and alert about how far one immerses oneself in one's emotions, passions and actions. Art is there to create a frame of reference. The analogy of masturbation occurs when one is so submerged in the 'act' of what one is doing that one perhaps forgets who one is, where one is, what one is doing, why one is doing it and who one is doing it to! One 'gets off' on the *intensity* of one's own release, the power of the feelings, mistaking them for some kind of great truth. There is absolutely nothing wrong with masturbation in the appropriate context (either on stage or in life). There is, however, something seriously wrong with rape and abuse in any context ... other than perhaps to demonstrate the wrongness of it.

And yet abuse happens all the time. This is one of the disturbing, ugly and disgusting abilities of the human race. If theatre is the mirror of society ... and if the actor is expected to explore these extremes ... how on earth do we deal with it? How can we go to extremes, be everything that we *are* spontaneously, freely, authentically, and yet know that we can pull out, back off, switch to another contrasting, opposite and wiser state of awareness when appropriate? Where is the control switch? How can we be totally immersed in the potential of who we all are and yet remain observant of how far we can go?

These questions quite naturally arise in the Playground. Where are the boundaries of who we are or can be in Theatre, in the Playground, as well as in Life?

The Edge ... there is no honest way to explain it because the only people who really know where it is are the ones who have gone over.

Hunter S. Thompson

In the Playground, as in Theatre, a conscious questioning of what one does both on stage *and off*, is pivotal. It is not about moral judgement. It cannot be. All good directors would expect a good actor to be able to engage with their feelings on all levels, to be flexible and go into any emotional state. In some cases the actor may be asked not to show any feelings at all, to show a neutral face in the face of disaster. At other times, being completely OTT might be artistic genius. Knowing the difference certainly is. On stage and in life.

In the profession we talk about economy and control.

A black-belt martial arts expert is capable of killing. S/he knows all the tricks. One look at a person with these skills is enough to sense that they are dangerous. We are talking about a form of 'self-awareness', which can only come from the experience of testing ourselves, our strengths and weakness in all extremes and in a variety of contexts, while observing the effect and the impact. The root of acting is ultimately *the ability to both expose and manage your feelings*, whether you are dealing with an improvised situation or a pre-written structured text ... or real life.

Acting requires a different form of intelligence. It requires that we 'exist' somewhere else, at the same time as acting, at the same time watching, witnessing, as it were, from a super-perspective. This is where we encounter the *self* that is *aware*.

Self-Awareness

Possibly more in theatre than anywhere else in life, actors become conscious of the ability to observe *oneself in action*.

The reader could try this now! Get up, from wherever you are reading this book, and take a step or two away from where you were just sitting or lying. Turn around and look at yourself as you were just now reading the book i.e. see your 'self' reading the book.

One becomes *an objective observer*.

In NLP, self-awareness is defined by *spatial positions* and *associated/dissociated states*. Spatial positions are places that one can literally, physically, step into; spaces from where one can view one's self from a different perspective, like a witness to one's own thoughts, emotions and actions. It is generally understood that we are more emotionally engaged in the associated (subjective) state. In the dissociated (objective) state we are less emotionally engaged.

I have observed that women tend to be more familiar with the subjective state; being socially and culturally permitted to be immersed in their emotions and feelings. Men tend to be more familiar with the objective state; being socially and culturally expected to not show their emotions; to be more detached, analytical and observant (certainly in Britain). In the Playground, I find that men tend to need to learn to be more subjective and women tend to need to learn to be more objective.

In acting we learn about both.

We learn that we can immerse ourselves in a subjective, sensual and emotional state, by *stepping inside an imagined picture*, rather like stepping into a 3D virtual world. In this associated state, we find ourselves identifying with the imagined reality directly, immediately and sensually, our emotions and feelings being awakened by the touch, sight, sound, smell and contact with our imagined surroundings in a very real way.

If we step *outside the imagined picture*, taking a step back from the screen as it were, we can watch the imagined drama or film unfold more objectively, in a dissociated state, rather like an audience does. This dissociated state does not exclude empathic understanding and feeling. The objective state can be as full of emotion as the subjective state, though maybe one step removed, more distant and less submerged in minute detail. One becomes more aware of the *whole picture*.

A brilliant Monty Python Flying Circus T.V. sketch I often refer to, when talking to the players about this phenomenon, is the one where a bunch of the Python comedians are crawling through the desert on all fours, exhausted, de-hydrated, nearly dying and then suddenly one of them says: '*Hey, wait a minute! Who's filming this?*' They all turn around towards the eye of the camera and realise joyfully that they can ask the camera crew for some water, which is what they do. The next shot is of the same Pythons, plus camera crew, all crawling through the desert on all fours, exhausted, de-hydrated, nearly dying, when again suddenly one of them says: '*Hey, wait a minute! Who's filming this?*' Again they all turn around to the eye of the camera and ask the camera crew for water … and so on and so forth.

Actors learn to see things not just from the perspective of the actor, but from the perspective of the camera crew and the director … all at the same time. We are creative observers.

> **But in its most archaic sense, theatre is the capacity possessed by human beings – and not animals – to observe themselves in action. Humans are capable of seeing themselves in the act of seeing, of thinking their emotions, of being moved by their thoughts. They can see themselves here and imagine themselves there tomorrow.**
>
> Augustus Boal, *Games for Actors and Non-Actors*

I never met or worked with the Brazilian theatre director, writer and politician Augustus Boal (1931-2009) sadly, but, as much as I love the above quote and totally admire what he contributed to society through Forum Theatre, I would probably have had to argue with him that I am not completely convinced that animals *can't* or *don't* observe themselves in action?

I saw a documentary once about some monkeys. I can't remember which kind of monkey exactly, there are so many different types, but they were sitting on a human rubbish dump playing with their favourite toys, which happened to be little bits of broken mirror. Each monkey sat and stared at their own reflection in their piece of broken mirror for hours on end. Fascinated, they seemed to be aware that they existed. They were conscious of themselves.

Animals, certainly mammals, clearly feel and dream (have we not all witnessed a dog chasing a rabbit in sleep?) and therefore probably also imagine like humans do. We can't exactly ask them what they dream or fantasize about. We can't ask very small children what they dream of either, because they don't have the vocabulary to describe it, nor perhaps do they know the difference between dream and reality. Maybe there isn't a difference. Personally, I would be very careful about saying that humans are the only higher primate or mammal that can observe themselves in action.

But point made. Adult humans can be perhaps more *aware* of their ability to see themselves in action than animals and small children are, despite the fact that we are not currently given opportunities to develop this skill in schools. Which is a shame, because the development of this type of *self-awareness* (as opposed to a shy self-consciousness) can greatly increase one's under-standing and management of one's behaviour and emotions.

Imagine! An actor is playing the role of Romeo, for which he has rehearsed a long time. He is performing to a large audience. He is supremely conscious of the audience in the auditorium with one part of his mind. With another part of his mind, he is immersed in a scene where he discovers that his beloved (Juliet) is dead. He decides to kill himself, because he can't live without her. A tragic moment, which requires the actor's greatest sense of truth, focus and conviction, if he is to *mesmerise* the audience and not turn the whole thing into a rather boring pretentious cliché. If he plays it well the audience will be *drawn into his reality* ... his subjective world. He captures their attention and holds it. He and the audience are connected through one imaginary vision. Everyone present is filled with suspended belief.

The audience, although objectively observing, is touched emotionally. It is perhaps a cathartic moment for some of the audience, because emotions are awakened, the heart beats faster and energy is released. I have experienced this myself, when watching excellent theatre.

At the end of the scene the two lovers are both dead, entwined in each other's arms. The lights dim slowly. The curtain falls. The applause begins and escalates. The curtain rises again for the curtain call and the lights brighten. Both actors are standing to take their applause ... their 'normal' selves again, happy, because they know that they have performed well.

With a flick of a light switch the actor can consciously change states.

In the profession, when acting, we say: 'I'm in it' or 'I'm not in it'. Let me explain what I mean by this. When I say: 'I wasn't in it', I mean I wasn't totally immersed in the role or the scene. I was conscious that something was missing. Some part of me wasn't connecting with the role in some way or with the other players. It didn't feel real. I didn't really feel it or engage with it. My heart wasn't in it. It was as if I was operating purely outside of myself ... perhaps just going through the technical motions. Doing what I was directed to do or expected to do.

When I am 'in it' I am immersed, totally focused, in an imaginative 3D world, as if it is reality. At the same time there is a connection between me, the actor, and my Self, the observer of my own actions. My Self has a connection with the audience too. I can feel that the audience is drawn into that imaginary world with me, temporarily suspended or lost in the same real time and space. It is difficult to explain.

In this imaginal mirror-like zone, *self-awareness* exists in a parallel space, watching what I do, so that I don't completely forget what it is I am actually doing and why! I guess it might be a bit like, in the jungle, where a part of the monkey that is watching out for danger, while the other part of the monkey is sleeping and dreaming.

In acting, we can become aware of both parts operating simultaneously. We can decide which state, or which side of the mirror we want to be in. Maybe monkeys are conscious of both parts too? Maybe they are conscious of much more than humans? Who knows what mysterious dimensions we all live in together? Which part of us is dreaming? Which part is sleeping or even 'sleep-walking'? Do we actually need to know? The more we probe, the more curious everything becomes.

> **How can you prove whether at this moment we are sleeping, and all our thoughts are a dream; or whether we are awake, and talking to one another in the waking state?**
>
> Plato, c.427-347BC, Greek philosopher

Of course we are not taught these things in school. We are told what is real and what is not real, what we are supposed to believe.

Memory and Imagination

Imagine a lemon in your hands. This is a well-known trick taught in the study of hypnosis and NLP. If you immerse yourself in the image of an imaginary lemon in your hands, you will be able to see the shape and colour of it. You will find that you can feel the outer peel of it with your fingers. You can both feel, see and smell it ... if you want to. Now try biting into it. You can taste the sourness in your mouth. If the visualisation is strong enough, the saliva glands in your mouth will actually start salivating ... reacting 'as if' it was real.

In a similar way one can recall feelings and physical sensations that are associated with past events, smells, colours, music, sounds, movements, people or objects in one's life. We immerse ourselves in the imagined and the senses awaken. It can also be that the passing smell of something or a particular sound will awaken a memory. There is a two way stimulus.

What is lesser known is that this is an acting technique called *Sense Memory*. Sometimes also called 'Emotional Memory', it is a highly effective tool used by some actors to recall and express various *peak emotions* on stage and in film (as, for example, the actor playing Romeo might have done in the tragic scene I just described). This technique was first introduced to the acting world by the famous Russian actor and theatre director Constantine Stanislavski (1863–1938). He recognised that the sensual awakening of past memories and/or the imagination of events that have not yet occurred, can cause very real physical manifestations, for example tears, laughter, blushes, pupil dilation; changes in the heartbeat, breath, spinal posture; muscle cramps and tensions; the swelling of blood vessels and/or a paling of complexion. These changes are not imaginary. They are visible to all and anyone who witnesses them. (I will be describing how to use this technique more precisely in *Games, Part 5: The Underbelly*.)

We observe that there is a two way stimulus between memory and imagination, as there is between mind and body. Another thing that many people don't realise is that:

Memory and imagination run on the same neurological circuits.

NLP presupposition

Memories are in fact not necessarily facts. Memories are our personally stored sensory perceptions of past events i.e. what we choose or select to recall, as and when. I mean, what happens if I suddenly realise or discover that I remembered an event 'wrongly'? I am sure we have all experienced this phenomenon. We ask: 'Did I imagine it?' 'Was I dreaming?' 'What was I thinking or feeling at that point of time that made me see/hear things that way?' It is confusing.

We have to ask: What part of our being was focusing on what part or aspect of 'reality' at the time? Another important question is: How can our perceptions in the now alter those choices?

Learning to act can take the player rapidly towards the realisation that we have the power to *change* our perceptions of the past and the future, both in negative and positive ways. The power lies in the way we *choose to see things*. Actors simply learn to question and exercise these imaginative muscles of choice.

In Chapter 5, I will be describing plenty of games that develop these skills on multi-dimensional levels.

Empathy and Imagination

... one of the most important functions of theatre in human society is to give us experience of situations that we do not encounter often enough in real life.'

Glenn D. Wilson 1994:18

What happens when a professional actor chooses to play a role that falls outside the actor's own personal range of past experiences or stored memory bank?

This is where imagination enables the actor to *empathise*.

If the actor can't identify with or get into the role by sensually awakening memories of past personal experiences, then s/he will need to conjure the unknown reality up by 'tuning into' the lives and experiences of others.

We can all do this (with rare exceptions). It would not be so hard for anyone to imagine what it would feel like to win the lottery! It gets more complicated when the actor has to, for example, imagine what it feels like to be completely drunk, if they never drank alcohol in their life. It is not difficult, but much more challenging to imagine the mental and physical horror of someone who has been abused, tortured or locked in an isolation cell for days on end. Or to imagine what it feels like to be interrogated as a witch two centuries ago or imagine what it feels like to give a king's speech with a stammer or even betray and murder someone for the possession of a crown or a beautiful woman. It may well be necessary to project into the future and imagine what it feels like to lose a child or the love of one's life, but some of the greatest dramas involve these dark themes, comedy and tragedy alike: grief, loss, betrayal, false accusations, jealousies, lust, cheating, tyranny, murder, incest, bullying and torture.

Some of these experiences can be found, recognised or *compared* with things that happen to us directly or indirectly, to varying subtle degrees, in our daily lives. Some players might have memories of *similar* things locked away inside. But if the actor has no experience of these situations at all, if they can't 'personalise' it, then s/he will have to imagine it or put him/herself into the shoes of someone who has.

> **Empathy is ... the mental entrance into the feeling or spirit of another person or thing**
>
> Living Webster Dictionary

An actor might have to go to enormous lengths to play a part convincingly, for example experiencing what it really feels like to be starving, by literally starving him/herself. Either way, the actor has to think, feel his/her way into the situation. One steps into it. One becomes one with it. One learns to empathise with the fate or destiny of others. One learns to look with new eyes at the extremes of life. Accomplished actors have the ability to see and feel things from a whole range of different perspectives. Their instrument can play many different tunes. Thus they acquire the ability to change frequencies, shape-shift and transform.

> **We perceive an object by 'resonating' with it, getting in synch with it. To know the world is literally to be on its wavelength ...This would mean that the art of seeing is one of transforming.**
>
> Lynn McTaggart 2001:108-9

I have to quickly add the obvious, in case there is any misunderstanding, that the Playground does not necessarily encourage anyone to get drunk or starve themselves in order to prove a point! That is the individual's personal choice. They have every right to do that if they feel it is necessary. Why not? These acting games *are* simply intended to push boundaries; to push the envelope; to challenge and encourage the players to go places they wouldn't normally go, imaginatively, sensually and experientially.

Acting is in the first instance about FEELING and SENSING what is going on inside and outside. This is what we explore in the Playground. There are of course other disciplines involved in professional acting, which are comparable to the mastery of playing an instrument e.g. memorising vast amounts of text off-by-heart; breathing correctly; creating vocal resonance and projecting the voice; precision and economy of movement; maintaining authenticity, even on repetition ... but primarily, it is about seeing, listening, sensing and feeling.

In the 'real' world we are encouraged to function far too much in our heads. We negotiate our way around our feelings mentally, verbally, cognitively, analytically, logically, avoiding the expression of real feelings or gut instincts. This avoidance is so chronic that we see the increasing emergence of pathological states of being, heart related disorders, panic attacks, irritable bowel syndromes ... not to mention all the other degenerative dis-eases.

In the Playground, we open the heart. The heart is associated with courage, openness, daring, passion, compassion, joy, love and truth. We reawaken our trust of our belly-brain, our gut feelings, which is associated with intuitive and psychic intelligence. Physical and mental blocks and inhibitions are removed. Memories are awakened. Pent up emotions are released. We are invited to see things and events from new or different perspectives. Simply by witnessing these revelations and transformations, being present to them and resonating with them, one's perceptions of life can be dramatically altered. These are *shared* experiences.

Here we come across the theatrical phenomenon of *Catharsis*.

Catharsis

> **(The word Catharsis) is derived from a Greek word meaning 'purification' and it refers to a release of tension that is supposed to follow from the powerful unleashing of pent-up emotions, induced by theatre (especially tragic drama and opera).**
>
> Glenn D. Wilson 1994:4

Aristotle used the word 'catharsis' at the end of the 6th chapter of his work De Poetica, which is the earliest surviving work of dramatic theory (335 BC): '*A Tragedy is filled with incidents arousing pity and fear wherewith to accomplish its catharsis of such emotions.*' The word catharsis has since then probably been the most analysed and redefined word in theatre, with several layers of meaning including 'cleansing', 'purification', 'enlightenment' and 'break-through'. Whatever it is, it certainly occurs with an emotional release of sorts, an unblocking of energy trapped within the body.

In the Playground, these breakthroughs are often associated with big 'Aha' moments of insight, enlightenment and clarity. And yet, it is the *removal of the blocks* that is the key factor.

> **... the things to get rid of or purge are not the emotions and desires, but on the contrary the blocks and repressions which inhibit us from fully experiencing and expressing our emotions and desires.**
>
> Dr Eberhard Scheiffele, award winning psychodramatist and psychotherapist. *Theatre of Truth* 1995:115-6

Acting investigates the *danger zones* of self-expression, the inhibitions, blocks and fears, which are common to all of us and which prevent us from connecting and resonating with the world in its full spectrum.

Breaking through these blocks and thereby releasing trapped emotions is usually a positively empowering experience. The removal of the block (or Mask) can potentially be 'exposing' and therefore initially frightening for some, so the process can only be positive if it is held and shared by all who are present in a safe, respectful and honourable way. That is the function of the Playground.

It is incredibly important for me to stress again that, unlike in 'real life' or in the acting profession, there is *no pressure* in the Playground. It is not about competition, achievement or any associated stresses. It's not about prescribing what is right or wrong for anyone. It's about PLAY ... simply testing the boundaries of what we think we know and becoming more emotionally intelligent.

Emotional Intelligence

What is emotional intelligence? Daniel Goleman (d.o.b 1946), American author, psychologist and science journalist, suggests in his book *Emotional Intelligence,* published in 1995, that resisting impulse is '*The Master Aptitude*':

> **There is perhaps no psychological skill more fundamental than resisting impulse. It is the root of all emotional self-control. Since all emotions, by their very nature, lead to one or another impulse to act.**
> Daniel Goleman (d.o.b. 1946) American psychologist and science journalist.
> *Emotional Intelligence* 1995:81

Controlling one's emotions by 'resisting' unwanted impulses may be very useful in the world we have been educated to believe is 'normal'; where politicians have shiny white teeth, soldiers are trained to kill and sportswomen/men compete to win gold medals.

Paradoxically, in the acting dimension we become aware that if we *resist impulses* too much, if we exercise *too much* emotional self-control, we will never get close to truth, to understanding what the root cause of an emotion or feeling is, nor its real potential. If you deny a feeling, how can you know what it is? How can you respond truthfully to it?

Removed from the threats of the 'real' world, in a theatrical setting, we can learn both. We can learn how to *resist impulse*; to pause, take a step backwards and think before we act...but also how to pick up and listen to emotional impulses, explore them, feel them deeply, intensely and *release* them without fear or shame.

Through experiential play, we realise quickly that we can be in two places at once; acting, at the same time witnessing oneself in action. I sometimes refer to this as *psychic bungy jumping*! One part goes deep into the emotion, while another part remains anchored, clear headed and detached. This increased *self*-awareness creates a safe reflective platform from which we can dive to the heart of the matter (even if only briefly) and return to, having recognised what these deeper emotions are truly trying to tell us.

GITTE, 33 YEARS OLD, DANISH: Gitte, a qualified nurse, had for a year been feeling confused, trapped and afraid of what would happen next. She was beginning to experience panic attacks and to isolate herself more and more. This was seriously impacting on both her work and social life. She came to the Playground in a desperate effort to gain confidence and find a new way forward.

During the games, Gitte was clearly trying very hard to be positive, to have fun and join in wherever she could, but it was also clear to me that she was blocking vital aspects of herself. Part of her couldn't play spontaneously, freely or openly. She was trying to be 'nice' and was very guarded about showing her real feelings.

A dramatic transformation occurred when she took part in a creative challenge that explored the *Sense Memory* technique (mentioned earlier and explained more fully in *Games – Part 4: The Underbelly*), where I asked the players to visit a specific emotion by recalling a moment in time when they remembered having felt that emotion quite strongly. The emotion I invited them to explore on this occasion was FEAR. Via a series of sensual questions about the remembered experience, Gitte was able to recognise that her feelings of fear had actually been masking, blocking a deeper layer of suppressed, but totally justifiable RAGE, which she allowed herself to feel and express for the first time deeply.

In the feedback afterwards, Gitte was able to open up to the group and explain that she had experienced a traumatic relationship with her first long-term partner, which had turned from romantic love to verbal and then physical abuse. There had been a long difficult separation and intermittent 'stalking'. He wouldn't let her go. She felt guilty and she blamed herself for everything. She was trying too hard to be nice and kind. The powerful cathartic revelation informed her that she had the *right* to be very angry indeed, to ask the police for help and to contact a lawyer. From then on she took the 'reins into her own hands' and transformed her reality from one of passive, confused self-doubt to one of confident, creative action. Instead of resisting natural impulses, she became intelligent about the impact of her deeper emotions and what they were telling her to do.

On another level, increased emotional intelligence (in the way that I define it in the Playground) actually allows us the real space and time to reflect on what emotions are. How do emotions arise? It is interesting how we can be confused about who or what is actually 'making' us feel things. We say: 'S/he *made* me feel so angry.' 'That song always *makes* me feel so sad.' As if one's Self had no choice in the matter.

If an objective yet integral part of ourselves witnesses from nearby or from afar; a part that is able to see the situation from another viewpoint, but clearly also empathises, feels, understands our inner truth ... then which part of us actually feels emotions? I don't have any universally applicable answers, but here is an interesting quote, adding yet another dimension to the way we can perceive 'reality'.

Richard Gere, Hollywood Actor and long-term Buddhist practitioner, said in an interview with Melvin McLeod (of Shambala Sun.com):

> I had been a Zen student for five or six years before I met His Holiness in India. We started out with a little small talk and then he said, "Oh, so you're an actor?" He thought about that a second, and then he said, "So when you do this acting and you're angry, are you really angry? When you're acting sad, are you really sad? When you cry, are you really crying?" I gave him some kind of actor answer, like it was more effective if you really believed in the emotion that you were portraying. He looked very deeply into my eyes and just started laughing. Hysterically. He was laughing at the idea that I would believe emotions are real, that I would work very hard to believe in anger and hatred and sadness and pain and suffering.

ShambalaSun.com

The Roles We Play

> (Improvisation or the ability to improvise) can assist in shifting the parameters in which we live. In bending the rules it proposes new forms.' (Frost&Yarrow 1990:180) '... the self is prised free of its encrustation in habitual role, and becomes an active producer of its own meaning.

Frost&Yarrow, *Improvisation in Drama* 1990:161

I need to distinguish here at least on one level between the 'real' and the 'imagined', although for me they inescapably merge. When I refer to *habitual roles*, I mean the everyday character(s) or personality a player assumes in order to fit in, survive or succeed in the 'real' world.

Examples of these roles could be: *the mother, the one that always looks after others first, the nurse, the quiet mouse, the perfect secretary, the nerd, the nice guy, the overworked solicitor's clerk, the victim, the alien or the outsider, the bad boy, the bad girl, the punk, the loose woman, the anarchist, the constant clown, the good sport, the life and soul of the party, the know-it-all, the teacher, the policeman(woman), the controller, the boss, the matriarch, the patriarch, the one that holds it all together, the self-acclaimed guru, etc.* We recognise some of these roles. There are many more. Most people embody one or more contrasting habitual role, which emerges in different contexts.

When I refer to *new roles*, I mean those that one hasn't played before.

Through a variety of acting techniques and challenges, I invite the player to dip and dive into as yet unknown aspects of his/her self, trying different archetypical parts on for size, as it were ... *the demon, the wise man, the pimp, the whore, the monster, the child, the tyrant, the murderer, the murderess, the drunken fool, the joker, the trickster, the prisoner, the jailer, the arsehole, the magician, the healer, the vampire, the parasite, the goddess, the angel, the saint, the snake, the witch, the monk, the priest, the rebel, the soldier, the hero, the fool etc.*

In the safety of the Playground the players can try out these new roles; how they interact with other parts or dynamics of the Self, as well as with other players in authentic ways and within a variety of familiar or unfamiliar contexts.

It is incredibly important for me to stress again that no player is pushed or cajoled into going anywhere they don't *want* to go. It just doesn't work like that. Sometimes the resistance to take on a particular role may be strong! For me this may be an indication of a potential block of some sort ... perhaps a hidden shadow or blind spot ... but the choice is theirs! The players are completely complicit in their own imaginative transformations. It cannot function in any other way.

The games called *Princess and the Potatoes; Stepping into the Picture; Precious Objects; Power Swops; Strange Encounters; Animal Envelopes* (found in *Games – Part 3 and 4*) demonstrate how this is possible.

The aim is not necessarily the discovery of a single or stable self in the conventional sense; it may be more the activation of a range of possible roles and modes, the discovery of the ability to play with one's own life.

Frost *et al* 1990:146

It is not about getting rid of the habitual Masks that we have so carefully created for our own personal safety and identity ... nor is it about the victim becoming an obsessive tyrant in the 'real world'. But if the 'quiet little mouse' discovers that she can be more flirtatious or more assertive, and if the 'eternal clown' discovers that he can express his fears, his vulnerabilities, without losing face, then we are talking about a mini revolution, which opens up a new and exciting vista of other possibilities in terms of viewing and interacting with the world.

Paradoxically, in this way one becomes more one's real self.

As the actor gains confidence by passing private barriers, the need to present a façade in society becomes less pressing.
Peter Brooke (d.o.b 1925), theatre director, *The Empty Space*

JUSTIN, 45 YEARS OLD, ENGLISH: Justin was unemployed and suffering from bouts of severe depression. He initially came across as a bit distracted, unkempt, and lost; some might suggest, a bit mad really. But, in 'reality', inside, we discovered he was just lonely, angry, confused, yearning for love and to be accepted as an intelligent, normal and complete human being. He now makes films, looks fantastic, dresses in drag sometimes and supports others in their spiritual journey through life, whatever that is. This is what he wrote, just a few weeks after having taken part in the Playground sessions:

'It's about passion I realise;
what I used to call madness.
Somebody told me it was unacceptable.
Now I've found this space,
This wonderful receptacle
This crucible, where I can be wild
Where I can go to the edge
And even plunge over,
Knowing that I'm safe,
Knowing that I'm loved.
It's a place where I can flex myself,
Where I can roar and pout and scream,
Where I can laugh and dance
With all those demons
That fill the stage with their implements
And increments of pain and celebration.
It is the dance of creation and destruction,
The Shiva two-step.'

Being Two-Faced

> **According to Greek mythology, humans were originally created with 4 arms, 4 legs and a head with two faces. Fearing their power, Zeus split them into two separate parts, condemning them to spend their lives in search of their other halves.**
>
> Plato

There are at least two sides to everyone. This is a 'generalisation' that I can safely state. In the acting dimension we know this. Actors play with opposites. This is what creates tension. This is what makes a character come alive; playing the opposite of what the role presents itself to be. If a character is described as evil, it can be far more interesting to play that role as extremely kind and nice, and vice versa! Heightened dramatic tension between two people in a scene can be created by changing the *subtext* (their inner thoughts) to the opposite of what is actually spoken (see *Subtext Games – Part 3, Authenticity*).

The willingness of any player to explore the opposite within their Self; to expose hidden aspects of their being, to 'come out' as it were, can be dependent on a variety of things ... for example, a player's relationship with the value systems of the society or culture that they grew up in. Those value systems can't necessarily be changed, but an individuals' *perceived dependence* on them can be explored.

GAVIN, 41 YEARS OLD, BRITISH. A self-employed carpenter by trade, Gavin was perhaps two stone heavier than he need be when he arrived at the Playground. He had short grey hair and soft, sensitive, grey-blue eyes. He seemed, on first appearances, like an 'average bloke', married, but with no children, stressed about work and struggling to make ends meet.

I was at first a bit confused by his being. He had a great sense of humour and imagination but, for some strange reason, when he improvised freely, his voice often retreated to a soft, trembling whisper that tailed off at the end of sentences. It was hard to understand what he was saying. It was as if he was swallowing what he really wanted to say.

Through a series of games and creative challenges involving *Body Instruments* and absurd conversations in *Fantasy Language* (both can be found in *Games – Part 2: Imagination*), I found out that he had, in fact, a beautifully resonating tenor voice and enjoyed singing in a choir as a hobby. Even so, his self-expression through normal speech continued to be muffled, swallowed or suppressed.

Gradually I got to know him better. In the Confidence games (see *Games – Part 3: Transformation and Truth*), where the Master has permission to boss the

Servant around mercilessly, I noticed that he played 'authority' with ease. He seemed to be very proficient at commanding others around effectively with a clear, strong, confident voice. I asked him how he did that. He said: 'That's my job. At work I have to be a man.'

The penny dropped. From that moment on, I encouraged him to explore more feminine roles and to dress as he wished. He lost two stone, grew his hair long and, when he came to the sessions, began to wear softer, more feminine styles and shapes, even a bit of mascara. As a consequence, he gradually became more outspoken and joyous, in a soft, sensual way. He was clearly much happier in his skin.

He began to explore the difference between being a man and a woman. For his 'One Minute Ritual' (see *Games – Part 4: The Underbelly*) he danced a martial arts dance for us, almost naked and covered in white paint. Thereby it was revealed that he also studied martial arts. The Playground provided Gavin with a safe space, which he clearly didn't feel he had in society at large, to become the mercurially androgynous being he really felt he was inside … all though I am aware that the Playground was only a part of his/her total liberation. Gavin told me recently:

> *I am (now) in 95% female presentation at work (albeit in practical work-ing clothes) and nobody has yet commented on it – rather odd really. Strangely I think that the people around me at work do 'notice' my transformation but make no direct reference to it – perhaps it seems natural and real … You, and the group that I started with, especially were a massive part of my transformation from a shy fearful state to something nearer to liberation and I found a whole new world through playing in this way. A fascinating journey that has barely begun – invaluable life experience!*

Blind Spots

> **Just as we have visual blind spots when looking at the road through our car mirrors, we also have psychological blind spots – aspects of our personalities that are hidden from our view.**
>
> psych-your-mind.blogspot.co.uk

Through watching the players dip in and out of unfamiliar emotional experiences and new roles, I have become particularly interested in the … *denial of the existence of parts of one's self.*

It seems that the existence of the *undesired* part negates or threatens the existence of the *desired* part. This is very tricky territory. How can one accept the existence of something that one doesn't want to exist? How can one see something one doesn't want to see?

We are not talking about Schizophrenia, although, from the perspective of the acting dimension, the concept or diagnosis of schizophrenia could perhaps benefit from a little rethink. There are quite a lot of things, in my opinion, that need a little rethink in what we call the 'real' world. For example, nature loves to create variety and within that variety there are cases of what appear to be *abnormalities*. And yet, hermaphrodites are born every day! In our Western culture they are usually quickly surgically transformed to either one gender or the other, which is a great shame, because the choice is clearly not the baby's and, one could say, violently invasive and discriminative. It seems that from many cultural perspectives hermaphrodites are not supposed to exist. The androgynous zone between the polar opposites of masculine and feminine is one of the biggest and most absurd taboos upheld in the world today ... and yet we all know that between the extremes of white and black there are countless aspects of a rainbow.

Despite anyone's ideas of what is right or wrong, I believe we all have the possibility of everything within us, including apparently conflicting opposites; the masculine and the feminine, the angry, the fearful, the good, the bad, the beautiful and the ugly, whatever one defines those things as being. We are all, in that sense at least *two faced*, probably *three or four faced*, which is fine. It's human.

What's dangerous is the denial of the opposite. It is through this denial that our hidden opposite more often than not becomes manifest in more destructive and subversive ways.

And yet, it's crazy to observe how some world players choose to remain vigilantly blind to the fact that something they openly hate, judge negatively, reject and point discriminative fingers at in others, may well be the very thing they suppress or don't want to see, recognise in themselves. This is how wars are created.

People can appear nice on the surface, convincing us that they are 'peace loving', while *secretly* harbouring thoughts of jealousy, ownership and revenge. The effect can be both internally and externally damaging. In the former, the suppressed emotions are trapped in the body. In both cases, they may find other more ominous ways to express themselves.

These are our *blind spots*. Like farts ... they are better out than in.

Blind spots are hard to detect, especially one's own, even though they are ubiquitous. We silence them. I find that the simplest and most effective way to find them is to set the cat amongst the pigeons. I encourage the players to play joyfully in the shadows, to flirt with the dirty, the dangerous and the wicked. To be naughty children. Break a few taboos. Actors love playing these games. It's very healthy for the Soul.

I might, for example, invite the players to play a well-known children's game: *Wink Murder* (with a twist), which involves people dying long drawn out OTT deaths at a wink.

This could be followed by the game *3 Deaths* ... which involves people inventing three highly imaginative ways of dying in rapid succession e.g. being strangled by a boa constrictor; dying of laughter; or falling over a cliff edge ... or *60 Seconds Death* (described in *Games: Part 2: Imagination*).

All three games end up as absurd takes on the reality of death and violence, which inspire hysterical laughter and very interesting and informative discussions.

It goes without saying that I would never introduce this type of game if I knew that any of the players were grieving or had a recent experience of trauma. Nor would any of these games be appropriate in the face of a national or global disaster. But, if and when appropriate, they might well fit the bill and give the players permission to explore their hidden shadows.

Another way to break a few taboos is to invite the players to invent their own fantasies of murder. For example, I might give them a short scene from a Hollywood blockbuster movie (see below) to inspire them. I explain that they can prepare the scene in pairs, with both players getting the chance to play both roles. They can *personalise* the scene by changing the names, gender, set interior/exterior, motivations and imaginative images that they are relating to ... or they can to stick to the basic elements of the script. It's totally up to them to find out what works best for them:

BULLETS OVER BROADWAY – Miramax, 1994. Screenplay by Woody Allen and Douglas McGrath. Directed by Woody Allen. (*Excerpt from 99 Film Scenes for Actors by Angela Nicholas – Avon Books 1999:42*)

INTERIOR. BILLIARD HALL – NIGHT.

CHEECH is helping DAVE with rewrites of a script. It's CHEECH's hangout.

DAVE: (*pause*) So what does it actually feel like when you, actually –

CHEECH: What?

DAVE: –   ki-kill a man?

CHEECH:	Feels O.K.
DAVE:	Feels O.K.?
CHEECH:	Yeah.
DAVE:	Even the first time?
CHEECH:	The first time? The first time was a punk in prison. He squealed on me and I stuck an ice pick in his back.
DAVE:	An ice pick?
CHEECH:	An ice pick, yeah. I had to do it over and over. Forty times, it was a mess, forget it.

It is fascinating what sort of alternative and controversial murder fantasies the players come up with; even suffocating their own grandmother with a duvet! Should we be shocked? Appalled? But, what about in everyday life? These are the scenes we hear about every day on T.V. news bulletins and in the blockbuster films we pay good money to see.

How do actors enact and re-enact such scenes? Imagine studying for the part of Lady Macbeth. How does one make such a murderous, treacherous and inevitably doomed character convincing? How did the lovely Johnny Depp manage to play the demon barber, Sweeny Todd, or Whitey Bulger in Black Mass? One has to search for an authentic reason to commit such crimes within oneself. What fun! What revelations one discovers about one's own human potential and those of others, who pose as our oppressors! How informative!

It is truly bizarre how funny and genuinely cathartic these simulations of dark material can be, when brought into the light. It is also interesting, how, in simple creative challenges like the ones I have just described, many players do indeed transform from being fidgety, evasive, un-centred, shadowy, nervous players to suddenly becoming attentive, alert, centred, still, dark-eyed and fearless.

It is as if they begin to sense their own inner strength and power for the first time; not for the dark, but for the potential of justice and the light.

Beyond the Mask

We create appearances. We construct ways of convincing others (and ourselves) that our outer presentation is the real one. It is the same in life as it is in theatre.

As I have already described earlier, it is therefore that skilled actors learn to be very conscious of the SUB-TEXT (see *Games – Part 3: Transformation and Truth*) – the motivations, thoughts and feelings behind the words their character speaks, i.e. what is going on behind the Mask. This is a dangerous subject. How to create illusions and how to break illusions.

In theatre, it is the *interplay* between mind and matter, between the Mask and the eyes behind it and beyond it, between the observed and the observer that is the most fascinating phenomenon of all.

> **We don't know much about masks in this [Western Capitalist] culture, partly because the church sees the mask as Pagan, and tries to suppress it wherever it has the power (the Vatican has a museum full of masks confiscated from the 'natives'), but also because this culture is usually hostile to trance states. We distrust spontaneity, and replace it by reason; the Mask was driven out of theatre in the same way that improvisation was driven out of music.**
>
> Keith Johnstone 1981:149

Knowledge of the power of the Mask is both ancient and modern. Cultures in all parts of the world recognise and use it as a device to invite a spirit or being into the body. In ritual they are part of a transformation: to create, amplify or fulfill the wearer's identity or sense of inner spirituality. They provide the wearer with the means to transcend their personality and enter an *alternate state of consciousness*. Looking through the eyes of an animal mask enhances an alternative awareness of the world ... yes, and even an ability to predict or see things that the 'normal' human can't.

Carl Jung (1875 – 1961), the renowned Swiss psychologist, introduced the word *persona* (which in Latin means Mask) into the field of psychology. He used it to describe the social face that the individual presents to the world: '*a kind of mask, designed on the one hand to make a definite impression upon others, and on the other to conceal the true nature of the individual.*' Jung also suggested that, somewhere behind the Mask, we have a second psychic centre ... *a second entity that is interested in truth.*

Truth, in this sense, I understand to be an inner objective voice; that of the unconscious intuitive self that knows far more than the conscious logical mind. Whatever this relationship is between the Mask and the wearer, or how it is perceived, it is indeed fascinating to experiment with ... as long as the person behind the Mask remains conscious of the fact that the Mask can take over!

We only have to read William Golding's *Lord of the Flies* to get a clear example, albeit fictional, of just how dangerous the Mask can be. Jack's camouflaged face transformed him from a choir boy to a savage capable of killing innocent Piggy, uniformly inspiring others to do the same. The Mask can offer the wearer a form of anonymity that allows an immoral aspect of their being to become manifest. In this sense, yes, it is dangerous.

Consciousness of this danger i.e. consciousness of one's potential Shadow, enables one to be less easily *taken over, controlled, hypnotised* or *entranced* by any unknown lurking predators of one's own psyche.

But there is more to this strange phenomenon. What is this thing ... this face of humanity? A Mask clearly transforms the *inner experience* and the *outer appearance* of the wearer and yet we know that the same beautiful face can be seen in different lights. We know that perceptions of beauty or ugliness, good or evil, lie in the eye of the beholder. What we see in the mirror, is not necessarily what other people see. Who is influencing who or what? Which part of whose dream of reality are we playing in or reflecting?

> **If faces were different when lit from above or below –**
> **what was a face? What was anything?**
>
> William Golding *Lord of the Flies*

How or why the phenomenon of the Mask functions is a curious subject; as inscrutable as the art of Hypnosis, where results are similar ... apparent for all to see, but with no real explanations for why or how these trance states occur. The effects cannot easily be verified *scientifically*, adding another threat of danger to the limited logical brain. If it can't be predicted or understood, then it cannot be controlled!

And yet knowledge of these 'bewitching' ritualistic skills has existed throughout history, in theatre, yes, but also in esoteric circles, whore houses, military operations, political arenas, royal courts, as well as in courts of Law. One doesn't have to look far to find evidence of the use and the abuse of this knowledge lurking somewhere, no less in the offices where the persuasive tactics of Consumer Marketing Industries are designed today.

Mesmerism

> **As modern science brings technological enlightenment**
> **to this world, it's high time to bring hypnosis out of the**
> **dark ages and shine the light of truth on its secrets.**
> **Let's rip away once and for all the shroud of mysticism**

**that has surrounded this art for so many centuries.
Let's begin by exposing the biggest secret of all; the
power is NOT in the hypnotist, it is in the client ... the
person who is guided into hypnosis!**

Roy Hunter, author and award-winning Hypnotherapist,
The Art of Hypnotherapy 2000:3

The moment a good opportunity arises, I explain to my players the basics of how hypnosis is understood to work. I explain that we are all, in fact, hypnotised in some way all the time. Rather like when we drive a car or read a book, we can in retrospect recognise that there were moments we were so immersed in thought or imagination that everything else seemed to disappear. We forgot what we were doing and can't remember how we got to where we are now. It was as if another part of our being took over and we have to ask ourselves *who* took over and where time went.

I explain to my players, it's important to know that through the use of a particular type of *focus and breath* one can very easily enter a self-induced trance state oneself. One is, in this case, both the hypnotised *and* the hypnotist!

In a similar way, using acting techniques, one can hypnotise an audience. By slowing down and giving the observers (the audience) enough space and time to dream, we allow them to watch us and imagine with us. Knowing where to place one's attention and therefore also the audiences' attention, by breaking normal patterns of behaviour, one can *stop time*, as it were, and literally psychically *alter the atmosphere in the room*. Through the power of imagination, the use of eyes, silence, timing and carefully placed gesture, we can literally draw the observer into a subconscious trance state with us ... a state of *suspended belief*.

In creative challenges like *Monologues from the Heart* (found in *Games – Part 4: The Underbelly*), where I coach the players in how to create their own imaginative bubbles, some players have described their experience as a conscious 'lifting out of the body'; also as a 'spiritual experience'.

After years of practicing and teaching the same thing, it is my experience that almost anyone can do this, once they have gained the confidence, the know-how and are given the freedom to practise it.

Saying all this, there is no doubt in my mind that, in theatre, the audience's *willingness* to be mesmerized or entranced is dependent on a few other factors as well, for example, the content of the play/film, the quality of the acting and the direction, the price they are willing to pay for the tickets and the fame (authority) of the leading actors.

Never-the-less, two things are certain: The skills and techniques employed by accomplished actors play an enormously important role in the relationship between the observed and the observer. Knowledge of these mesmerising techniques enables one to *claim the power of choice* [Hunter 2000:19] ... i.e. one becomes aware that one can choose to be hypnotised or not!

In the next chapter, I include numerous examples of different types of creative challenges that are aimed at developing ones imagination in relation to time, space, attention and intuitive intelligence. They deepen the player's understanding of *the relationship between the observed and the observer*, while introducing at more and more advanced levels increased *self-awareness* and a *consciousness of one's power of choice*.

Through receiving this knowledge and engaging in this type of play, the players begin to rethink much of what they thought they knew and much of what they had been taught in school. They begin to *notice and see things they hadn't noticed before*. They begin to make their own connections between their inner imaginative world and the outer manifestations of that world around them. The invisible becomes visible.

> **I had a major epiphany going back to the car. A joining up of dots ... the first dot was what we talked about: that self-criticism, doubt and negativity is just as much the work of ego ... the second dot was my increasing sense, and many have said the same, that to make good art, the ego and cherished preferences have to get out of the way, in order to allow the work to unfold ... my epiphany, (so obvious now!) is that it's not just the ego work of self-importance/inflation, but also the ego work of self-doubt and negative judgement that has to get out of the way. I sat in the car and was stunned for five minutes because it's so simple and I hadn't seen it before. I saw a powerful lesson today!!**
>
> Player's testimony

The Shadow

> **Our deepest fear is not that we are inadequate. Our deepest fear is that we are powerful beyond measure. It is our light, not our darkness that most frightens us.**

Marianne Williamson, founder of The Peace Alliance – *Return to Love*

The ability to split ourselves into two parts, the conscious and the unconscious, the good and the bad, the selfish and the selfless, negative and positive forces, feminine and masculine, the visible and the invisible, seems to be an innate human strategy for creativity, survival and transcendence. There is no reason why a split should not exist. It seems that the eternal war of opposing dynamics is a part of our integral nature, our evolving dramatic story and the drive that carries us forward in the universe. But, it all goes horribly wrong when blindness sets in ... blindness to one part or the other.

> **The key to understanding how Nazi doctors came to do the work of Auschwitz is the psychological principle I call "doubling": the division of the Self into two functioning wholes, so that a part-self acts as an entire self.**
>
> Zweig&Abrams, *Meeting the Shadow* 1991: 218

The 'Shadow' or 'Double' is another term that Carl Jung introduced into the world of psychology to describe the unconscious inner opposite of the more conscious exterior.

In principle the theory describes how we can be as blind to our beauty, our generosity, our selflessness, as we are to our selfishness and narrow-mindedness. The suppression of the inner opposite can result in a tragic denial of our true worth, as well as a horrific form of scapegoating. The latter is what the Nazi's did to Jews, the Church did to so called 'witches', the colonialists to 'primitives', the white slave owners to 'blacks' and Victorian supermen to 'hysterical women' and 'disobedient children'.

We shun, criticise, enslave and annihilate what we understand to be value-less, inferior or undesirable, both within us and outside of us. But, *'when the superior man tries to repress the inferior man, within or without, he forces the latter into revolt.* [CW 11: Psychology and Religion: par 136, pg 79]

For those who are not yet familiar with this subject, I can highly recommend the book *Meeting the Shadow* – an insightful collection of writings, compiled and commented on by Connie Zweig & Jeremiah Abrams, about the hidden power of the dark side of human nature. The writings include those of Carl Jung, Robert Bly, Joseph Campbell, James Hillman, amongst a host of other exceptional minds. It is certainly one of the books that I recommend to players in the Playground. For example, James Hillman writes:

> **At once something else must break through, that laughing insight at the paradox of one's own folly which is also everyman's. Then may come the joyful acceptance**

of the rejected and inferior, a going with it and even a
partial living of it. This love may even lead to an
identification with and an acting-out of the shadow,
falling into its fascination. Therefore the moral dimension
can never be abandoned. Thus is a cure a paradox
requiring two incommensurables; the moral recognition
that these parts of me are burdensome and intolerable
and must change, and a loving laughing acceptance
which takes them just as they are, joyfully, for ever.
One both tries hard and lets go, both judges harshly
and joins gladly. Western moralism and Eastern abandon:
each holds only one side of the truth.

Hillman, Meeting the Shadow, Zweig & Abrams 1991:241

Meeting, exposing, owning and embracing one's own and the communal Shadow has become central to the evolution of the Playground.

It is fun and fascinating, but not always easy. The Shadow is a delicate subject, which I approach with caution and respect, precisely because there are very few absolutes in my world. And yet, I have watched how players bravely claim and dance with their Shadow, their inner opposites, fears and projections, with good humour, perhaps for the first time, and somehow find much peace with that. I would not dream of launching into a major discussion with them about it ... only if they indicated that they wanted to. The intimacy of these revelations can be deeply personal matters that have been exposed in trust. All one has to do is observe them, indicate silently through empathy that they have been seen, heard, felt, respected, and allow them to be. Some things are better left unsaid. But, I do ask players to watch their dreams.

When the shadow becomes *conscious of itself* ... for that is, in fact, all it needs ... the other 'parts' of the *whole gestalt being* begin to converse in new ways with each other. Conversations show themselves in the form of new roles, new masks, archetypes, signs and symbols, roles and relationships, in the players' dreams, in their imaginative play and in the 'real world'.

Whether a player chooses to articulate and share what they have discovered in words or not, the positive transformations clearly manifest in non-verbal ways. Players begin to relax and grow in inner strength. The spine visibly straightens out and the face muscles look softer and calmer. The eyes are deeper, more open and still. The player focuses better, is less fearful, has a greater sense of humour and demonstrates a more caring and gentle awareness of others. They begin to shift and change things in their lives in a beneficial way for themselves and for the people around them. They take responsibility for their own *actions*.

If individuals know that they should have love, respect, self-respect, and so on, they can consciously seek them out. Certainly everyone will agree that seeking them out consciously will be better and more effective than trying to make up for their lack unconsciously.

Abraham Maslow 1970:103

The Creative Gaze

It was not a matter of asking whether the source of hallucinations is internal or external but of considering that it might be both at the same time.

Jeremy Narby, d.o.b 1959, anthropologist, *The Cosmic Serpent*

Before we close this chapter and move on to the Games, I'd like to very briefly introduce two professional theatre practitioners; Declan Donnellan and Michael Chekhov, whose teachings and techniques include important insights into how 'the way we see things' affects our actions, our emotions and states of being. The majority of what they teach is specifically dedicated to the art of the *professional actor i.e. 'stage worthiness'*, but again one finds crucial parallels, which are applicable to life in general.

Declan Donnellan (born 1953) worked as associate director of the National Theatre and for the Royal Shakespeare Company. He also formed a company of actors in Moscow. He teaches '*Who I am is what I see.*' [Donnellan 2005:84] and that an actor has to be highly sensitive to what is 'out there'; the target of their vision. He describes how we have to authentically tune into, listen to and respond to what is around us, but our response is determined utterly by what we want to see, what we choose to see, and by which aspect of the totality we choose to zoom in on.

Does the actor playing Juliet choose to see that Romeo loves her or is she afraid that he might not love her? Playing with these opposites makes his/her acting come alive. Donnellan explains that life itself comes in opposed twos:

There is no night without day. There is no honour without shame. And a declaration of love is terrifying because the joy of being loved back must exactly mirror the terror of being rejected.

Donnellan 2005:52-3

In life, we play these doubles all the time, whether we are conscious of it or not. How aware are we that our anger or frustration is driven by a fear of failing or not being accepted? Each moment is affected by the tension between our dreams and fears, an all or nothing dynamic between the two extremes of satisfaction and disappointment, succeeding or failing, being accepted or being rejected. *'Actors can unleash tremendous energy after grasping that humans must play these doubles'* [Donnellan 2005:74].

This concept combines beautifully with the *Chekhovian* ideas that I am particularly fascinated with. You see, there is yet another mysterious layer to all this seeing, believing and imagining.

> **At night when we are alone in our bedrooms, sharp images often emerge from the darkness. Before our mind's eye the events of the day mysteriously disappear. The faces of people we have seen, their conversations and mannerisms, the streets of a city or the fields of the countryside suddenly reveal themselves. Mostly, we look passively at these familiar pictures, but among them appear strange visions, unknown to us. Scenes, moods, events, and people with which we have no connection intermingle with our everyday mental images and branch out in all directions. The new images seem to develop and transform themselves independent of our control and wishes.**

Chekhov 1991:1

Michael Chekhov (1891–1995), Russian-American actor, director and author was, I think, one of the greatest acting teachers of all time. He coached visionary actors like Marilyn Monroe and Clint Eastwood. Anthony Hopkins and Jonny Depp have both cited Chekhov's book as being highly influential on their acting. His concepts about the Psychic Gesture are described in his book *On The Technique of Acting*, where he teaches about the interplay between the conscious and the unconscious mind.

Chekhov teaches that one can access clues to characters (roles one might choose to explore and play) by entering a transpersonal realm; a realm of the imagination that transcends or reaches beyond the personal or individual ... what Jung describes as the *collective unconscious*. The word "transpersonal" comes from the Latin "trans," meaning beyond and through, and "persona," meaning mask or personality.

We can all enter this realm, via our imagination, not just in dreams, but in conscious waking states! Chekhov refers to this technique as the *creative gaze*.

They saw what they wanted to see, and in this lay the power of their "gaze", but they also enjoyed the independent activities of their images, which transformed themselves under their questioning look, acquiring new qualities, feelings, desires, manifesting novel situations, symbolizing new ideas, revealing fresh rhythms.

Chekhov 1991:4

Because of this interplay between that which we consciously seek and our collectively and unconsciously connected yearnings, surprising things can reveal themselves through the creative gaze. It is 'as if' we are communicating in this transpersonal realm with something far greater than our Self, but common to us all.

We say in the art of acting that one is only as good a player as each other. What I give is what I receive. And vice versa. Accomplished actors learn to be very *generous*, to be intuitively in tune with, listen to, feel and be aware not only of their own desires, fears and needs, but also those of other players, characters and roles. *We are all vital parts of the whole play*. Together we create the whole picture that manifests before our eyes. Together we create the world we live in.

Now for the games!

You can discover more about a person in an hour of play than in a year of conversation. – Plato

CHAPTER FIVE

THE GAMES

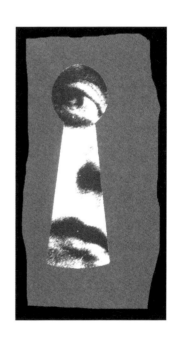

THE GAMES DESCRIBED in this chapter (which is divided into four parts: *The Approach; Imagination; Transformation & Truth; The Underbelly*) are by no means a complete collection of the resources I have developed for the Playground. The ones I have selected are intended to give the reader a *flavour* of the experiential process and its potential.

It may be superfluous to add that all the games described here are intended for adults (18 years plus), although many of them are also brilliant for younger people and children. I know this from experience, as I have taught younger people many times. Some could be, certainly would need to be adapted for younger minds and audiences. Others are not suitable at all. This book is primarily written for adult players!

I intend to go into as much detail as possible ... perhaps too much detail. Over the years, I have developed a particular way of describing the games, techniques and concepts, which seems best to meet the players' understanding. Forgive me if I explain the obvious, but rather that, than leave the reader or the player floundering.

I'll be mentioning where the games were sourced (if I can remember!) and adding notes and more case studies where applicable, in order to clarify how they best function. Occasional options for advanced versions will demonstrate how one can expand on ideas and techniques.

It is important to note that none of the following creative challenges need to be played logically in the order laid out in this book! I hope it goes without saying that one doesn't have to complete everything in *Games – Part 2,* before moving on to Part 3 and 4 etc. The main aim of any play session is to provide a variety of experiences that meet the needs and abilities of the constellation of players that are present.

No session is ever the same twice. A typical session will have a combination of highly physical games to loosen up, go mad, de-stress and de-mechanise, balanced by games that induce qualities of stillness, intense focus, reflection and inspire thought provoking discussions. One important tip I can give any facilitator is that ... diversity and change are definitely key ingredients. Don't get stuck in one game or concept for too long. The transformational process works best, when the players move quickly from one state of mind to another. At times they need to be utterly silly. At other times they need to go deep, reflect, feel and dream. Sometimes they need to be encouraged to scream, stamp, roar, shout or tremble and share enlightening revelations ... but then bounce swiftly back to absurdity and laughter again. I try to create an exponential dance that explores the extremes of life and being.

There is, however, a very special way of sensing what should or could come next, which only a facilitator who has experienced the complete Playground process would be able to begin to intuit. I am including some guidelines for the facilitation of the Playground at the outset in Games – *Part 1: The Approach*, which will give a clearer picture of some of the facilitation skills required. Even so, even though one *thinks* one understands some of the ideas that I present in this book, this does not qualify one to teach or lead a session involving games and concepts, which took 40-50 years direct experience for me to understand. If someone would like to train as a Playground facilitator, they would need to complete the process and receive additional instructions from me.

THE GAMES
Part 1: THE APPROACH

> **Common sense and a sense of humor are the same thing, moving at different speeds. A sense of humor is just common sense, dancing**
>
> William James, 1842-1910, psychologist and philosopher.

THIS FIRST GAMES section is all about creating a setting that facilitates trust, warmth, safety, group bonding, openness of mind, the taking of risks and, of course, a sense of humour. Having said often enough in this book that there are no rules ... there are of course a few down-to-earth, practical, common-sense guidelines which may sound ridiculously obvious, but they need to be stated before we can proceed to the warm up games.

FACILITATION

> **Do not train a child to learn by force or harshness; but direct them to it by what amuses their minds, so that you may be better able to discover with accuracy the peculiar bent of the genius of each.**
>
> Plato

My approach is very positive and encouraging, no matter what happens *(see foot note). I try not to make comparisons. I make it clear that everyone is unique and yet all are the same at heart. Everyone develops at their own pace and the players' breakthroughs and discoveries are relative to their needs. I praise everyone and explain exactly why I am praising them. My heart tells me *never* to criticise, unless someone asks for *constructive* criticism, in which case I might suggest what they could try to focus on next time, in order to make the game more rewarding for them self and everyone else. I openly admit that I don't always get it 'right'. I try to give plenty of time for feedback and discussion.

There is only one ground rule. No-one should *intentionally* or *consciously* hurt another player. Accidents can happen. We are all human. But they are less likely to happen if we use basic common sense. Other than that there are no rules ...

except perhaps within the context of a particular game, but even there, once the players have grasped how that rule works, I encourage them to break it! There are no exams, no contracts, no awards and no failures. There is no competition or race. No deadlines. No fixed end-products. There is always time for everything. There are no pressures put on anyone apart from the demands that a person would put upon themselves, perhaps because they know they have more within them, which I totally respect. There is no stress. It's rather lovely really.

I have to openly admit that there have been occasions where I have had to ask a player not to return to the Playground. It is usually because of 'attention seeking' behaviour that persists, no matter how much attention they receive, or because they bring a negative and threatening energy to the group. These situations are extremely rare. In fact, this has only happened twice in 40 odd years of teaching!

The Setting

The Playground does not need to take place in a fully equipped theatre, although that can be fun too. Nothing is excluded. It could take place in someone's living room or in the open air or in a ruin with fire-light and pure abstract imagination shadowed and reflected all over the walls.

When I use the word 'stage' I am referring to an open space or clearing, where the players have room to play ... in contrast to the audience zone where others can sit and view the play. Both are moveable. The stage does not have to be a raised platform. I choose to use the word 'stage', because the Playground concept is rooted in the ancient and sophisticated wisdom of theatre i.e. *the place where you view*, but I encourage the players to remember that 'all the world's a stage'.

The stage, for me, is a place of utter enchantment and suspense and needs to be respected as such, at all times, as it does in real life. When a player steps into the stage area, anything, including that which is sometimes called 'magic', can happen. And yet, at the same time, at some point, we begin to realise, that there are no real or rigid boundaries between the stage area and the audience zone ... or even between the playground and the outside world. Where are these imagined boundaries? It is a matter of perception. I have players who come to me, even after just a few sessions and say: '*The world seems like a different place out there now. It feels like everything is a potential drama.*' [Student testimony]

It is, however, essential that the Playground sessions take place in a safe and relatively quiet space, with enough room to go crazy and get physical. It does get quite loud sometimes, with shouting and laughing, so the space one chooses should be out of earshot of neighbours who might feel disturbed by it. It's important that the participants don't feel uncomfortable about letting go of their inhibitions.

It's great if the space is equipped with enough seats for everyone in the group, maybe a couple of small card tables to use for some scenes and loads of cushions to chuck about or fall on. It's brilliant if there are facilities for making tea or coffee in the break. It's also nice if it's warm, although some settings after the Wall came down in Berlin, were not warm at all! We didn't have chairs, tables or cushions, but that didn't seem to stop people playing. We just put thick coats on and imagined the rest!

Group Numbers

The groups, or constellations of people I play with, are rarely more than ten, in fact nine is better. This is very important, because the discovery process doesn't seem to function optimally with large, oversized groups. I believe this is because people need a small intimate group to bond with. If given permission, people are self-selecting. Sometimes a group will start with 11–15 participants. After a couple of weeks, a few will leave quite naturally of their own accord, so that the group invariably whittles itself down to anything between six and nine, which seems to be the perfect size. It's sort of magic.

For the process that I am writing about in this book, I'd like the reader to keep this ideal 6-9 constellation in mind.

Sometimes I separate out the Beginner, Intermediate and Advanced levels, but usually the groups are made up of mixed abilities, because we can all learn from each other.

Time Frames

The complex lives and unique individuality of each player has meant that the discovery process I have designed for the Playground is very loose. Non-linear. It's more like a spiral, with a beginning, but no end, where players can drop-in and out, revisiting the games and the concepts at more and more advanced levels, if they choose. Some return to the process again and again over years of sporadic play.

In the Playground there are no time limits, other than those that fit in with the practicalities of the players' everyday lives and work demands. Some players prefer one regular weekly session of 3-4 hours (which they describe as the high-light of their week!) Others prefer the occasional intense weekend workshop or are attracted to a week retreat of play, as an alternative holiday. In this way, the groups and the time limitations create themselves.

Please note that, when I refer to a 'session' in this book, I am talking about a three hour session (with a 15 minute break half-way through) that takes place on a regular once-a-week basis.

Sharing

I tend to come with a very flexible game plan. Everything and anything can change very quickly. The players may arrive with a whole range of anxieties or concerns from their 'real' lives, involving personal encounters, private grievances, hurts, losses, joys, new love affairs, sudden financial burdens, family conflicts, problems at work or physical ailments that have occurred during the week. I would be completely mad not to take any or all of those manifestations into consideration before starting to play ... hence the concept of a sharing circle before we begin. It is not about 'therapy'. In any setting, professional or other, this form of sharing should be a given. Our troubles and concerns should never be left outside the door (as they are often expected to be in a professional context). They should be shared. It is pure common sense.

Therefore, in a seated circle, before we begin, we briefly discuss how we feel and what our expectations for the session might be. It does not have to take long. In this way, we open up the possibility of taking care of each other and I get a feel for the games that would be most appropriate. Similarly at the end of the session, I create a circle again to discuss what the players have seen, observed and are taking away with them.

The ability to say 'NO': At the beginning of the process, and on a regular basis in the sessions (in conjunction with the subject of confidentiality), I make sure that the players all know that they can say NO to anything I invite them to do. They can *refuse* to join in with any of games and challenges, if they want to. In this way they learn to respect their own judgement and trust their own *intuitive* instincts. They can sit and watch and listen if they like, which is also very inform-ative. They are permitted to create their own boundaries and in doing so, learn and earn the right to respect the boundaries of others. It's as simple as that. This is the first step towards building or regaining self-belief.

The ability to say 'YES'. Having told the players that they need to be able to say NO, I invite them also to be curious and open to saying YES, especially to challenges that would normally make them freeze or block or run in the other direction. Explaining this prepares them for one of the primary techniques in improvisation, which I describe later: ADVANCING IDEAS – a 'Yes, and ... ' technique that ensures players expand on imaginative ideas (see *Games –Part 2: Imagination*).

WARM UP GAMES

After sharing, we warm up physically and psychically in crazy ways. Warm-ups are about *inducing another state of consciousness; breaking patterns; de-mechanising fixed habits; scrambling the logical brain; entering the intuitive body i.e. generally getting into the zone of spontaneous play, joy, openness and generosity.* The idea is to de-stress the whole being and draw the players into the NOW.

In a three hour session, the warmup could be anything between 5-20mins.

What I find works best is giving the players a series of guided challenges that are fun, childlike and, above all, *unpredictable*; things that are, initially, as silly as possible and that stimulate the imagination in mad, unexpected ways. I choose things that get the players' hearts beating and breathing deeply (relative, of course, to the abilities of the whole group) ... a series of actions and random focusing challenges that *interrupt habitual patterns* and generally *scramble the brain*. We are in the first phase of *de-mechanisation*.

For example – we start with a good physical, all body shake-out and then a group run around, involving filling the empty spaces, hugging, jumping up and down, freezing occasionally and looking each other deep in the eyes. I say that the walls of the room are moving inwards, so we all have to get closer and closer ... and then the walls expand outwards again. After that, I might get the players to move together like shoals of fish or water swirling around rocks (the other players being the rocks). I might suddenly ask them to run around and scream like children in a playground, or be balloons or bumper cars bumping into each other (safely), or to fly like sea gulls or bats out of hell, or greet each other like long lost friends or robots ... Strangely enough grown-ups love doing this sort of thing.

I encourage the players to use their voices as much as possible, without worrying what they sound like. I join in, because it's fun, but mainly to show them how extremely silly, stupid, child-like, uninhibited and adventurous one can be. Once they get the hang of it, and some individuals *do* get the hang of it very quickly, they become the new pioneers of eccentricity.

Suggestions for these initial spontaneous activities are too manifold and varied to be included here, but hopefully some of these ideas give a feel for what is possible.

Getting the Giggles: More often than not, new participants get the giggles when they are playing these sorts of child-like games, or when they are looking deeply into someone's eyes for the first time. They may even continue to get the giggles in some of the more serious, stiller and tenser improvisations later on. This is perfectly normal. In my opinion it is fantastic! It is a sign that their inhibition and fear is being expressed and releasing itself. I never make a big thing of giggles. I simply remind them that actors love to do very *very* silly things. I never, *ever* make someone feel that they are doing something wrong if they laugh! Given time, I can assure you, the giggles transform into a very different form of serious focus and attention.

Peripheral Vision: When the players are moving around, I encourage them to explore peripheral vision ... looking out the corners of the eyes, which actually induces a trance state of awareness. One becomes more aware of everything in the room, as opposed to detailed targets. I encourage them also to look up and out, rather than down on the floor. I suggest that they can see out the back of their heads! In this way their unconscious spacial instincts start taking over ... which is safer.

After the initial shake-out, heart-pump and group run-around, which should have got the players into a joyously intuitive state, one might want to add a few *psychologically strategic* warm-up games. These are either based on ancient children's games, picked up in the professional acting world or invented by myself. The idea behind this type of game is to begin to introduce a few absurd rules in order to encourage illogical and non-competitive team-play. Here are four of the players' favourites:

LOVE/HATE CHASE: I ask the members of the group to choose one person in the group they hate (not really) and one person they love (not really). On the word GO, they chase after and try to cling to the person they love, while keeping as far away as possible from the person they hate. This inevitably ends up in wild, miscellaneous swirling patterns of unusual behaviour with a lot of scream-ing. I tend to play it 2-3 times, each time asking them to choose different players to love and hate, in order to see what strange patterns of movement manifest.

Note: Depending on the energy present in the room, the participants *might* have to be reminded to take care of the participants who are not as strong and agile as others. Once mentioned, they usually work this out for themselves.

THE KNOCK-KNEE CHAIR RACE: I was told that this is one of the warm-up games played by professional actors at the Globe Theatre, in London. It is highly exhilarating.

First one should count the number of participants, plus the facilitator (who takes part). Let us say ten players in total. Place ten chairs, evenly distanced around the room. Nine of the players sit on nine of the chairs ... leaving one empty chair at one end of the room. The one remaining standing player goes to the other end of the room (the opposite end to the empty chair) and promises to keep his/her knees firmly locked together (i.e. knock-kneed). S/he starts to walk (with difficulty) towards the other end of the room with the aim of sitting in the empty chair. As s/he gets closer to it, one of the seated players will have to decide to leave his/her chair and sit in the empty chair in order to prevent the knock-kneed player from sitting in it ... which means that his/her own chair is now free. The knock-kneed player then heads off towards the new empty chair ... in which case another seated player has to leap towards that empty chair and sit in it ... leaving yet another new chair free. The knock-kneed player then heads off towards the new free chair ... and so forth. The aim is to stop the knock-kneed player from sitting anywhere. If s/he manages to finally sit in an empty chair, then the player left standing gets to be the next knock-kneed player.

Note: The other nine players are not knock-kneed!

MINISTRY OF SILLY WALKS TAG: Ridiculously stupid and an all-round quick warm-up and release, this game is based on the famous Monty Python sketch with the same name. The person who is 'it' i.e. the player who chases and tags the others, has to decide on a silly walk. S/he proceeds, walking in this imaginatively silly way, to try to catch the other players. All of the people being chased have to imitate his/her silly walk, while trying to run away from 'it' ... until one of them is caught. That person becomes 'it' and invents a new silly walk, which the others imitate ... and so forth.

TAG WITH SONIC VARIATIONS: I recently discovered this warm up game in a book for professional acting called *The Outstanding Actor* by Ken Rea.

The players start playing a simple game of tag, but the new 'it' cannot tag the player who caught them for five seconds after being tagged. They have to tag someone else. This rule continues throughout the game. After playing this simple version for a short while, the facilitator starts adding sonic variations e.g. the person who is 'it' has to:

1. make a continual noise of some sort until they tag someone. That person then becomes 'it' and has to make a different noise, until they tag someone else, and so forth.

2. sing a song of choice until they tag someone. That person is then 'it' and has to sing a different song until ... etc.

3. be a 'kung fu' fighter with appropriate sounds and movements until ... etc.

4. speak in fantasy language (a.k.a gibberish or googledy-hoopf) ... etc.

Note: This game develops physical centeredness, agility and vocal control, while moving strenuously. (For an explanation of what Fantasy Language is, see *Games – Part 2: Imagination/Fantasy Language*)

DE-MECHANISATION GAMES

After the warm-up games, the players are ready to use the *spoken word*, although we are still in the first phase of *de-mechanisation*. Words tend to fire up the logical brain, so what we are now going to do is to seriously scramble the logical brain in preparation for the more focused imaginative challenges, which come a bit later (*Games – Part 2: Imagination*).

I need to add that the process of disorientating the logical mind is something one may need to return to at various stages of the process, because the logical mind loves to take over and dominate! Therefore, my de-mechanisation games come in two forms, *simple* and *advanced*.

I'll start with the simple de-mechanisation games and move on to the more advanced ones later (in *Games – Part 2: Imagination*). The simple ones can be used as an extension of the warm up, the advanced in conjunction with more advanced games. All of the de-mechanisation games function in a similar way to the art of *hypnosis*, in that they dis-orientate the analytical part of the brain, making conversations with the unconscious, intuitive part of the mind increasingly possible.

I do not want to take advantage of the naivety of the players in this context, so I always explain to the players how *de-mechanisation* functions:

> **Life can become a series of mechanisations, as rigid and as lifeless as the movements of a machine.**
> Augustus Boal 1992: xxv

I explain that humans operate far too much from a perspective inhibited by logically indoctrinated analysis (what we learn in school). We are too much in our heads. De-mechanisation games scramble the players' brains with the effect that they find themselves letting go of preconceived or adopted ideas and enter a more 'belly-brain' orientated, intuitive and imaginative state of being. In this state they will become more conscious of their feelings and gut instincts, as well as being more open to new creative ideas.

RANDOM WORD CUSHIONS: I invented this game, which is based on some of Keith Johnstone's ideas. One needs about 3-4 soft cushions (or bean bags or balls). Everyone stands in a large inward facing circle with plenty of space between them. I start by chucking a cushion at one of the players and saying any random word loudly ... e.g. *custard*. That person then does the same, throwing the cushion at another player and saying another random word loudly ... e.g. *telephone*. This carries on, throwing the cushion faster and faster between the players, all saying words without worrying what comes out ... *custard, telephone, bug, fart, turtle, lunatic, doughnut, tree, dog, blue, penis, ghost, freedom, electric* ... each word emerging as the cushion is thrown. Once it really gets going, I add the other cushions gradually into the game ... until literally a word/cushion fight develops with 3-4 cushions flying all over the place, sometimes two cushions hitting one person at the same time (in which case they have to throw two cushions and say two words). The words get ruder and more random. Everyone absolutely loves this game. In fact, it's quite hard to get them to stop playing it, which is fine.

Note: I encourage the group not to use *'associated'* words e.g. garden – hose – water – drink – glass – window – curtain – draw – paint – picture etc. This is important! We are trying to *de-mechanise* reactions, language and thoughts. But, if associations or repetitions occur, it really doesn't matter. There are no fixed rules. The aim is simply to be as random as possible. It's also absolutely fine if the words start getting rude. This is all part of the freeing up of the mind; permitting entrance into the *underbelly* and the *shadow* zones, which is one of our main goals. It represents a gradual undermining of an overly polite censoring process that corrects what we might otherwise spontaneously come up with.

Advanced Version: Ask the players to say two words at a time e.g. *custard pie*. And then later three words at a time e.g. *custard pie fight*. But each new combination should be randomly created!

DAILY REPETITIONS: Here's a highly physical brain scrambler that I invented. It is slightly complex, so it's best to describe it in stages:

Stage 1: I ask the players to think of three things they said that day ... short phrases, exclamations, comments, requests or queries. If they can't think of anything they said, they should just make things up e.g.:

    1. 'Pass the marmalade, please.' 2. 'Taxi!!!' 3. 'I can't believe it!'
    1. 'Where have you been?' 2. 'Cup of tea?' 3. 'It's down the corridor.'
    1. 'I said: Fuck off!' 2. 'That wasn't a joke!' 3. 'Have you seen my socks?'

Stage 2: When they've all got their three phrases, I ask the players to invent and rehearse an exaggerated or crazy physical gesture for each phrase, which they can repeat while saying the sentence demonstratively out loud over and over again. The gestures are best when they are quite extreme and absurd. I demonstrate some possibilities, so they get the hang of it.

Stage 3: I ask the players to designate a number 1, 2 or 3 to each sentence/gesture and a different place in the room for each sentence/gesture e.g.

      1. In the right corner.
      2. In the middle of the room.
      3. Near the door.

Stage 4: I explain that when they hear a loud whistle, they should all group together very quickly in the middle of the room and stand very still and quiet... until they hear a NUMBER (either 1, 2 or 3) called out. When they hear the number, they should all run to that number's designated place in the room and start repeating the sentence/gesture over and over again until they hear the whistle again ... which is the signal to go as quickly as possible into the middle of the room and wait for the next number. They carry on doing this, getting faster and faster, until they are all really quick, agile and good at it. At first they may totally forget what they are doing, which is great ... but they get better at it. The brain is learning to multi-task in new ways. New synapses!

    Note: A loud sports whistle is necessary, because the players get very loud and they need to hear the signal to go to the middle of the room. Some players end up having chosen the same designated space for the same number, but they work it out somehow together! No worries.

Stage 5: After they have all done this together as a group, you can get each individual player to show their three sentences and gestures to the rest of the group. Certainly by now, they are all well-rehearsed and will have reached a high point of abandoned expression that is very entertaining! They all enjoy seeing what everyone else has created and tend to laugh and applaud.

TRUST and TRANCE GAMES

Once the players' brains are scrambled to a degree, one can, for example, guide them through some *Trust and Trance Games*.

    Trust Games require feeling, sensing, a letting go of fears, physical closeness, and touch of some sort, which facilitates group bonding and mutual support. *Trance Games* invite a deeper layer of *unconscious activity* to come to the foreground of the play. Both require a slowing down and involve one of a pair or all people *closing the eyes*.

BEEP BEEP: This is a great game for trust and group bonding. It has a *trance-like effect*. All the players are asked to stand in an inward facing circle and close their eyes. I explain that I will come around and tap each individual on the head, one after the other, but in no set order. When the player feels the tap on the head, they should start making a vocal sound or 'signal' and begin to walk around the room, still with their eyes closed, while repeating their signal. (I tend to tap the most confident members of the group first!)

The vocalised signal can be anything like 'Beep Beep' or 'Hallo a lo a lo' or 'Dooo da doo da' or 'Brrrrr Brrrrr' or 'Fuck off' or 'Miaow' or 'It's Meeeee!' or 'Aunty Gemima' or 'Honk Honk' ... as long as it's different from everyone else's. Again, the sillier the better. I assure the players that, although they have their eyes closed they won't bump into anyone, because they will hear each other's signals as they walk around the room.

Once they have all been confidently moving around the room in this way for a while, I ask the whole group to find their way towards the centre of the room ... still with their eyes closed and making their individual vocal signals. When they get to the centre, I invite them all to cling onto one another, forming a large 'blob'. I invite them then all to move around the room together as a 'blob' or an 'amoeba' ... still with their eyes closed and all making their vocal signals.

At some point, one can ask them to increase the volume of their signals, but keep moving round the room like a blob. (At this point, they will probably all start smiling, because it really is very silly). I ask them to get louder and louder and then softer and softer again ... coming to stillness ... all ending up clinging together in a huddle, somewhere in the room. The last little signals fade out with intermittent chortling and giggles. Finally, after a moment of complete stillness and silence, they can open their eyes! This is when they all realise who they were hugging and where they are ... and invariably burst out laughing.

Note: The facilitator does not join in with this game, as there needs to be at least one 'open eyed' person to make sure no-one bashes into walls or furniture!

LEADING THE BLIND: This is another excellent game for building *trust* and *group alertness*. I have no idea anymore how or where I was introduced to it, but it has proven invaluable ever since. The players play in pairs (A and B).

A closes his/her eyes and is blind. B leads the blind A around the room by vocalising a signal or sound, which A follows. Similar to the Beep Beep game, the vocalised signals can be anything enjoyable and inventive, but distinctly different from anyone else's.

The signal sound is first established so that A knows what sound they are going to follow and then ... off they go. It is very important that B leads A *safely* around the room, making sure s/he doesn't crash into any other players or walls or furniture! This means that B will have to use peripheral vision (looking out the sides of both eyes) to keep a constant eye out for what everyone else is doing around them. B really has to be on their toes, in order to prevent A colliding into other players! After a while they swop roles.

Note: It's important that A keeps walking forward in the direction of the last signal, knowing that another signal will come again in time to turn them around and stop them bumping into anything! At first B makes the signal close to A, and at regular intervals, in order to build trust. As A's confidence grows, B can try distancing him/herself further and further away from A, repeating the signal after longer and longer intervals of silence. This really does take quite a lot of trust and courage. Needless to say, this game has to be done slowly and intuitively or it becomes virtually impossible. It's a good idea to discuss the impact the game had on the various players afterwards.

Advanced Version: I once played this game with a group of professional actors, some of whom decided to be jokers and intentionally make their blind partners bump into other players. It became an advanced form of 'bumper cars', which should really only be played by super confident players, who are not worried about health and safety regulations!

BLIND MAN'S BUFF: This is an ancient game, to which I have added another component and an adult twist. It involves two players that are relatively equal in size, age and strength. The two players are blindfolded. The rest of the players stand around the edges of the room and watch out for them. The two blindfolded players are first disorientated, so they don't know exactly where they are in the room ... after which they then have to try to find or hide an object that I place somewhere in the room.

The object I use for this game is a plastic bottle of sorts, with a few coins in it. The plastic makes it unbreakable and relatively soft. The coins ensure that it rattles and can be heard when it moves. I place it, with a demonstrative rattle, close to one of the blind player's feet. That blind player invariably finds is first, if not almost immediately. The other blind player has to find the player with the bottle and try to get it off him/her.

Note: Sometimes it's necessary for the facilitator to step in and give the bottle a little 'buff', thereby indicating where the player with the bottle is! Otherwise the player with the bottle might decide to keep perfectly still and silent. The game could go on forever!

It is wonderful to watch the blindfolded players struggling to find or get away from each other around the room ... sometimes missing each other by a hair's breadth. When they do come into contact, they roll about on the floor, wrestle and intertwine in ways that are often *totally uninhibited* in an effort to grab or hide the bottle. This game is very cathartic and exhaustingly entertaining. It is also very revealing about the individual player's personality and strategies for 'success'!

THE GAMES
Part 2: THE IMAGINATION

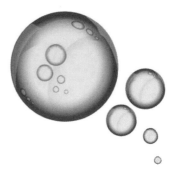

IN THIS SECTION I describe games that develop the imagination and remove creative blocks. They invite discussions about why and how we censor our creativity. They explore how we can creatively expand on ideas, whilst observing the *two way impact of mind and body.*

Mind/Body Games

> **The human body and mind are inseparable. No work of the actor is completely psychological nor exclusively physical. The physical body of the actor (and character) must always be allowed to influence the psychology and vice versa. For this reason, all of the actor's exercises must be psycho-physical and not executed in a mechanical fashion.**
>
> Michael Chekhov 1991: xli

BODY INSTRUMENTS: I created this game to explore the players' flexibility of body movement, their range of vocal resonance and the effect all this has on the freedom of the mind and imagination ... and vice versa. The resonances and vibrations of the body are all subtly linked with feelings and emotions. Once the players are immersed in this game, as strange as it sounds, they tend to be reluctant to stop. It's also an excellent preparation for the *Fantasy Language* games (which I describe a bit later).

The players play in pairs (A + B). A is the instrument and B is the player. A closes his/her eyes (and keeps them eyes closed as long as the game lasts) while B plays A like an instrument. Let me explain.

B touches various parts of A's body, to which A responds with a resonating sound and accompanying movement from that part of the body. For example: B touches A on the nose. A then moves, jerks, sniffs or wiggles the nose in a variety of ways, making nasal sounds, while exploring all possible movement, feelings and resonances possible in the nose (yes, it's weird!). A continues to do this until B touches another part of A's body e.g. the tummy. A then explores the feelings, sounds, movements and resonances in the belly for a while … until B touches another part of the body e.g. the centre of the back, the calves, the eyebrows, the toes, the ears or the top of the head etc.

Obviously we do not include sensitive or private parts in this game, even though there is a resonating quality to every part of the body, even the arse hole, the eye lids and the hair follicles. Every part has unique feelings. It takes a bit of imagination, but each part of the being can develop a 'character' or quality of its own.

Note: I usually have to demonstrate how it works for both A and B. I show B (the player) how they can get as large a range of resonating sounds and movements out of A (the instrument) as possible. It's good to get the instrument to lift and swing the arms about, as this frees up the ribs and lungs. The instrument can also be encouraged to relax more and to move about the room. Watch out for the other players though! And don't forget that silliness is a gateway to freedom. We are not trying to produce elegant, nice, pleasing or beautiful sounds … although they are not excluded. The aim is to be as free as possible, both in bodily movements and sounds. Soft sensual murmurs, rumbling roars, hums, sighs and groans, whistles and whines are all excellent. Animal sounds, like barks, purrs, twitters and high pitched screeches are cool. Operatic arias, orgasmic gasps, yodels, giggles and nauseous retches are totally wonderful too.

EMOTIONAL SYMPHONIES: This idea came from Augustus Boal's book, *Games for Actors and Non-Actors*. He calls it 'Emotional Machines', but I'd rather get away from the idea that humans should attempt to be or are machines. (It was after all Boal who advocated de-mechanisation!) Hence the new name – 'Emotional Symphonies'.

This game involves the whole group playing together to create a *rhythmical sound/movement* which has various emotional qualities e.g. FEAR, SADNESS, HATE, LOVE, ENVY, DESIRE, LONELINESS, GRIEF, JOY, VANITY, VICTORY, LUST, REVENGE, TIMIDITY, REJECTION, DISGUST etc.

Once a quality or emotion has been decided upon, for example FEAR, one of the group members starts first in the centre of the room with a sound and a rhythmical movement representing FEAR. The rest of the group watches for a short while. S/he is then joined by a second player, who adds a different vocal and rhythmical physical representation of the same emotion. They are free to move around the room, wherever they want to go. Gradually, one by one, the whole group joins in, until there is a complete orchestra of emotional sound, rhythm and movement, interacting in the whole space.

Note: If the players are ready for it, they can be encouraged to use the technique of *Sense Memory* (*Games – Part 3: Transformation & Truth*) to connect more deeply with the emotions.

FIVE TRANSFORMATIONAL STATES: This game is an eternal joy to watch from the perspective of facilitator or audience member. I explain to the players that they are all to play together as a group. No-one is leader. They have to follow each other. Using their individual imaginations they are invited to transform together in sequence into *five different given qualities or states*. I give the running order of the five states, which they all have to remember together. Here are a few examples:

1. Children in a playground
2. Seagulls at a seaside resort
3. Exotic fish in an aquarium
4. Worms under the earth
5. A forest of trees at midnight

OR

1. An electric shock
2. A swarm of bees
3. Blood corpuscles flowing in a vein.
4. Autumn leaves blowing in the wind
5. One large quivering jelly

OR

1. Fireworks exploding
2. A flock of birds
3. Waves crashing against rocks
4. Concentration camp inmates shifting rocks
5. One large creaking iceberg

Note: There is no time limit. The players can take as long as they want to transform from state to state. Some states will require that they play separately, in their own little imaginative bubbles, while other states will require that they are bonded or flowing together in some way e.g. in the case of the electric shock, the quivering jelly, the iceberg, the crashing waves, the shoal of fish or the blood corpuscles. Each transformational sequence evokes a different feeling, some of which admittedly are absurd and funny, but the combinations also include qualities of emotional beauty or tragedy too. As you can see, we are gradually beginning to introduce more emotional states. And, of course, I always encourage them to breathe and make the appropriate sounds with their movements!

FREEING IMAGINATIVE BLOCKS

We are now going to look more specifically at the different ways to develop the imagination. First, I am going to suggest a couple of creative challenges, which clarify exactly what imagination is and open up a discussion about the way we censor our imagination, our ideas and feelings (all of which are intimately linked).

> **Many students block their imagination because they are afraid of being unoriginal.**
>
> Johnstone 1981:87

1-2-3 WHAT DID YOU SEE?: In order to demonstrate that the players all have the ability to conjure up imaginative ideas or visions out of nowhere, I ask the whole group to close their eyes and, on the count of three, to see an object in their 'mind's eye'. Without giving them any further time to think about it, I quickly say: '1 – 2 – 3. What did you see?' I then get them to tell me in turn what came up for them e.g. a light bulb ... a pig ... a £5 note ... a grand piano ... a bucket ... a door ... a zebra crossing ... a sparkly ball ... a monkey ... a packet of garden peas ... sun-glasses ... a tree ... a little horse with a model cowboy ... etc. I haven't met anyone who can't do this yet.

Everyone with what we describe as a 'normally functioning brain' seems to have easy, instantaneous access to imagination. Imagination is simply the ability to see things with the *inner eye* and the trick is not to intellectually analyse it or question it. Just remember that the *first* thing that comes into your head is genius! You have to love and *trust* whatever comes up. Sadly, in school, we are so often given the feeling that what we create, dream and imagine is not good enough. 'Do it again, but do it properly.' Keith Johnstone explains how he was once crippled by fear of not being clever enough.

> **I forgot that inspiration isn't intellectual, that you don't have to be perfect. In the end I was reluctant to attempt anything for fear of failure, and my first thoughts never seemed good enough. Everything had to be corrected and brought into line.**
>
> Johnstone 1981:17

LISTS OF RANDOM WORDS: This next creative challenge lends itself to being played in a quieter, more reflective moment and acts as a prelude to a deeper discussion about how/why some individuals tend to censor themselves more than others. This may be a vital discussion for people who feel they are struggling with being imaginative at the outset of the Playground process. I'll describe this challenge in three stages:

Stage 1: The players take an A4 sheet of paper and a pen and I ask them to write *a long list of random words*. They have 2-3 minutes to write as many words as possible. Please note – this is not a competition about who can write the most words! The words do not have to be associated or rhyme or form sentences, unless of course someone feels like breaking the rules! Everyone has poetic and creative licence. But, for this game, I encourage them to simply write down *any word that pops into the head* as quickly and fluently as possible. They should just keep writing until I ask them to stop. If they have a mini mental block, they should simply put a 'dot' in that space, close their eyes and let the next word/object pop into their mind ... and then keep writing. After a couple of minutes, I ask them all to stop.

Stage 2: The players are invited to read their lists of words out. I encourage them to stand in front of the group to do this, but only if they feel comfortable with it. Remember that no-one *has* to do anything. It may be that some players feel shy or embarrassed about the words they came up with. It may also potentially be the first time that they have been invited to stand in the stage area *alone* in front of the audience! If they wish, they can read it from the viewer's area ... if they want to. They may not want to read at all!

During the recitations, everyone begins to observe that each individual player has a completely different list of words and that each list paints a very different picture of the inner workings of the creator's imagination. Each list is equally fascinating, though completely different in theme, structure, range, rhythm and emotion. At the same time, each player (who reads out loud) has a different presence, a different voice, a different posture ... a different sub-conscious world.

Note: As facilitator, I know that this represents only the ripples on the surface of much deeper things to come.

Stage 3: The individuals share their observations about the various recitations and are invited to comment on the moments where they perhaps 'went blank', where they had to put a 'dot'. It may have been a moment that s/he consciously or unconsciously decided *not* to write a word that came up, which opens up the potential for discussion, perhaps over a tea-break, about how and why we censor our imagination and therefore also suppress vitally creative parts of ourselves. For example, here are some ideas to inspire discussion:

CENSORING AND PERFECTION: Much of this subject relates to what I wrote about in *Chapter 3 – Invisible Walls*. There is clearly a link between our striving to be perfect in a world that dictates to us what perfect is and the censoring of vital parts of ourselves that are deemed to be stupid, imperfect, immoral, uncontrollable, weak or unnecessary.

During the discussion, I love to tell Carl Jung's personal story, which I found in his autobiography *Memories, Dreams, Reflections*. One day, as a young man (and son of a devout vicar), Jung came out of school and became overwhelmed by the beauty of the new golden roof of the cathedral in Basel, shining in glorious sunlight. As he stood looking at this beauty, his imagination suddenly witnessed something plummeting out of the sky and landing on the glittering roof. For a long time he refused to acknowledge what it was that had fallen from the heavens. It seemed so abominable to him and in the eyes of God that such a thought or image should enter his mind. Finally, after much confused inner searching and debate, he gathered the courage to open his imaginative mind:

> **I gathered all my courage, as though I were about to leap forthwith into hell-fire, and let the thought come. I saw before me the cathedral, the blue sky. Gods sits on His golden throne, high above the world – and from under the throne an enormous turd falls upon the sparkling new roof, shatters it, and breaks the walls of the cathedral asunder. So, that was it! I felt an enormous and indescribable relief.**
>
> Jung 1963:56

Thus began Jung's ground-breaking and giant universal theories about the relevance of the symbolism in dreams and waking visions. And thus begins the players' life changing journey of discovering how easy it can be to improvise.

Before I describe some very simple playful games and creative challenges that step by step lead the player to quite advanced improvisational skills, I need to explain the basic concept of ADVANCING IDEAS. As a challenge, it may at first sound perhaps daunting, even impossible, but all will become clear!

ADVANCING IDEAS: Knowledge of how and when to say YES and NO to the development of imaginative ideas is one of the most rewarding skills in spontaneous play ... and probably the most vital in LIFE! Both answers, YES and NO, have the possibility of taking ideas and actions to another conscious level. Experiencing the impact of the chosen options and playing skilfully with them can be crucial for human survival. Let me explain the concept and give some examples.

As mentioned earlier, I encourage the players to say NO, whenever their gut instinct tells them to, because the ability to say NO is important in the building of confidence, self-respect and the *creation of personal boundaries*. However, saying NO can also be linked to a fear of being silly or not good enough; a fear of the consequences of expressing one's imaginative thoughts. In some situations saying NO is appropriate, but in other situations it may be limiting and plain boring. By censoring our imagination, we may block the potential of genius creative play, not just for ourselves, but for others too. On the other hand, saying YES, may be downright stupid and dangerous. So, how do we know when to say: YES or NO? Only through playful imaginative experiences, in a safe setting.

The technique of *blocking* and *advancing* ideas has been described excellently by Keith Johnstone in his book *Impro* (see *Recommended Books* at the end). In the Playground, I use some of Johnstone's ideas to develop conscious and courageous creative choice.

Rejecting (or blocking) ideas goes a bit like this ... there are two players (A + B). A starts with an imaginative suggestion:

> A: Let's go for a swim in the river!
> B: Eeeer ... No.
> A: Oh, go on!
> B: What river?
> A: There!
> B: Uuuuh ... are you mad?
> A: Put your glasses on – it's there! Right there in front of us!
> B: I don't need glasses.

In this scenario, B is rejecting A's three offers i.e. 'going for a swim', 'there is a river right there' and 'B needs glasses'. This improvisation could *potentially* go in various directions. It could be that A really is mad! But, for the case of this example, let us say that A *isn't mad* and his/her imaginative offers have been *blocked* by B. B is perhaps afraid of appearing mad his/herself if s/he goes along with A's imaginative ideas (i.e. B has projected his/her own fear of madness onto A). In which case, the impact on A (and the people watching the scene) might well be disappointment and frustration. It could become excruciatingly boring if B continues to block A's ideas and doesn't offer anything better.

Accepting (and advancing) ideas goes a bit like this:

> A: Let's go for a swim in the river!
>
> B: YES, and ... let's go in completely naked!!!
> *B immediately pretends to take his/her clothes off.*
> *A decides to take his/her clothes off too*
> *... but then stops and thinks ...*
>
> A: NO, but … hang on a minute ... is it safe in the dark?
>
> B: Of course, it is! I always do this! A mid-night swim! Oh, by the way – the little black things are my friends!

In this scenario B has not only accepted A's offers, but has advanced them by expanding upon them. S/he suggests going in naked in the pitch dark. A takes it to yet another level of danger and suspense by mentioning the little black things. One can imagine what might happen next! It could get really scary or end up as a comedy prank. The choice is theirs. Together they have taken the action very rapidly to a whole other level, with both YES, *ands* ... and *NO, buts*. Both A and B are supporting each other to create an exciting, imaginative and highly entertaining improvisation, which could potentially go anywhere and which the observers love.

Experienced players learn that they have the choice of going in any creative direction they want. They can say both YES and NO. They can counter, block, advance, lead, follow, sometimes completely contradicting themselves and twisting the story in unpredictable ways. This is a great skill, which can be exercised creatively in life too.

Inexperienced players, however, tend to initially block ideas. It's a habit, born out of the fear of making a fool of themselves. So, in the beginning, I encourage new players to simply try saying: 'YES, and ... ' to everything!!! In this way, I get them to generously support the evolution of everyone's ideas. It is only play. Once they discover what fun it is, there is no looking back.

THAT'S RIGHT, BOB, and ... This is one of the players' favourites and is an excellent beginner game for introducing and practising the concept of advancing ideas by simply saying YES, to everything. They work in pairs (A + B). There is only one rule: After A has made the opening statement, they both have to keep saying *'That's right, Bob, and ... '* while continuing to add new ideas.

Note: They are both called Bob, no matter what gender!

A: It's a lovely day, Bob.

B: That's right, Bob, and ... what an incredible view!

A: That's right, Bob, and ... here we are up in the sky.

B: That's right, Bob, and ... the hot-air balloon ride was a great idea of yours.

A: That's right, Bob, and ... I thought you knew how to fly it!

B: That's right, Bob, and ... I thought I did too.

A: That's right Bob, and ... we've been up here for days.

B: That's right Bob, and ... nights.

A: That's right Bob, and ... I'm starving (*and so on and so forth*).

WHAT'S THAT? Once the whole group of players have grasped the concept of conjuring up imaginative objects and visions out of nowhere and evolving ideas together, they can practise their genius playing skills with this game.

All the players play together at the same time, but they play in pairs (A + B). A starts off by asking B: 'What's that?' (S/he points to an empty space, somewhere in the room). B answers immediately, drawing upon something from the imagination i.e. B doesn't literally say what A is pointing at! If A is pointing in the direction of a radiator, B shouldn't say 'That's a radiator.' B might say: 'It's a 'handbag'.

The 'thing' could start as a 'hand-bag' and, through a series of provocative questions and answers that both A + B come up with, the hand-bag might become e.g., a meat-eating death trap. The thing could start as a 'dog' and become the three-headed monster from Hades. It could start as a 'puddle of water' and become an ice sculptured castle in which A + B are both trapped, so they end up having to make a fire to get out. It could start as a 'hole in the road' and become a tour of mysterious underground caves. It could start as 'a potato' and become a trip to Planet Spud to get some chip implants. The inventions are endless.

After about 2-3 minutes of creation (things develop very fast in this game) I invite them all to stop and tell the rest of the group what became of their imaginary objects. Everyone is pretty amazed at the variety and the extent of other people's imagination.

Important Note: The more *physically active* the players are, the more their imagination tends to expand. So, I encourage the players to take up as much space in the room as they can, while playing this game ... and, at more advanced levels, even to leave the room and continue their imaginary escapades out on the street!

PANDORA'S BOX: This game was inspired by watching a professional Impro Group in action and adapting it for the Playground. It takes advancing ideas to another level. It is now possible to *reject* every idea that's given, i.e. say NO, thereby encouraging the other player to constantly think of something new *at a very fast pace.*

All the players play together at the same time, but they play in pairs (A + B). Between each pair is an imaginary box. A says to B: 'What's in the box?' B reaches into the imaginary box and brings out an invisible object and says what it is e.g. 'It's a cauliflower.' A then rejects that offering e.g.: 'Yuck! Don't want that. What else?' B then immediately (without complaint or objection!) reaches into the box again and brings out another invisible object and says what it is: 'It's a frog.' A rejects it again e.g. 'Ha ha. Load of rubbish. What else?'

> B: A large rock.
> A: What else?
> B: A pair of frilly nickers.
> A: Don't be silly.
> B: A golf ball.
> A: Chuck it away. What else?
> B: A pig's liver.
> A: Fuck off.
> B: A book.
> A: What kind of book.
> B: A comic book.
> A: Put it back. What else?
> B: A Boa Constrictor.
> And so on and so forth. A and B then reverse roles.

Note: This game is about *rapid fire*. There should be no time to 'think logically', so the faster the better. It is propelled forward as much by the emergence of objects as it is by the rejection of those objects. When this game gets up to speed, the players cannot be stopped. It becomes like a stream of consciousness. It is a brilliant way of training the 'imaginative muscles' and it can be played at almost every session, until the players become super confident in tapping into this form of invisible creation.

THAT'S NOT HOW THE STORY GOES! This game combines evolving ideas through both *acceptance* and *rejection*. Again the players play together, but in pairs (A + B). A starts to tell a story:

> A: Once upon a time, there was a knight on a horse riding
>   around the mote of a Castle ...
> B: NO, he wasn't.
> A: NO, he was riding around an M5 roundabout.
> B: NO, he wasn't.
> A: NO, he was riding a donkey through a desert.
> B: YES, and then what happened?
> A: He suddenly heard voices.
> B: NO, he didn't.
> A: NO, he felt very peculiar in his stomach.
> B: NO, he didn't.
> A: NO, he thought his head was exploding.
> B: YES, and then what happened?
> A: It exploded.
> B: NO, it didn't.
> A: NO, his mobile phone rang ...
> And so on and so forth.

Note: Needless to say, the person playing the B character can accept or reject whatever s/he wants as being relevant or not relevant to the story that is unfolding. The story can go on forever and, if it is not stopped, it will. The pairs then reverse roles.

THE THIRD ELEMENT: I really have no idea anymore where I got this idea from, but I thank whoever or whatever it was that inspired me. This game has been immeasurably useful and fun to watch over c. 30 years of playtime. It's a game that beginner players can enjoy in a very simple way and can be repeated throughout the process with increasing levels of advanced challenges.

Two players sit or stand on stage (the others watch). No direction is given. The two players are *not* told *who* they are, *where* they are, *what* they are doing and *why*, nor *when* it is. They have to make it up. All of this information emerges through the spontaneous conversation they have, through imaginative offers and advancing ideas. Initially, the conversation is based on the one rule of simply *accepting and evolving ideas*. The only direction I give the two players (at this stage) is that they should try not to go into the situation with any preconceived ideas. They should slow down and start from a feeling of emptiness and neutrality. Any ideas for creative inspiration should come from an inner feeling ... an authentic gut instinct; a spontaneous idea in that moment. Here's an example of what might happen:

A and B are both sitting facing the audience. They do nothing for a while, just feeling the energy and checking each other out. The expressions on their faces gradually begin to reveal what they are both feeling and thinking.

> A: *Looking more and more worried.* Have you told her yet?
>
> B: *Clearly watching telly and getting more and more ecstatic about something.* GOAL!!!!!!
>
> *There is a long silence, in which A's and B's contrasting feelings escalate.*
>
> A: *Shouting.* I SAID HAVE YOU TOLD HER YET?!
>
> B: NOOOOOOO!! Why did he do that????!!! The referee just gave him a red card!!!
>
> A: *Gets up and turns the telly off.*
>
> B: *Amazed.* Why did you do that?
>
> A: Have you told your mother that you're gay.
>
> B: *Looking sheepish.* No, not yet.
>
> A: You promised me.
>
> B: *Silence.*
>
> A: She thinks you're marrying a girl!
>
> B: *Silence.*
>
> A: SHE'S ARRIVING ANY MINUTE!!

It has become vaguely clear what is happening. We now know roughly *who* they are, *where* they are, *when* it might be, *what* they are doing and *why*. At any point from now on a 'third element' could be introduced either by the players or the facilitator. The third element has the power, like a bomb shell, to dramatically shift the direction of the improvisation. Here's a list of things that could happen now, which I, as the facilitator, could call out as a given direction or more advanced players could spontaneously invent for themselves. For example:

> The telephone rings.
> There's a knock on the door.
> A brick flies through the window.

There's suddenly a nasty smell in the room.
The fire alarm goes off.
A letter is pushed under the door.
One of the players has a heart attack.
One of the players starts hysterically laughing.
The table moves all by itself.
A baby starts crying.
A strange face appears at the window.
An angel appears with a message.
One of the players starts throwing a tantrum.
One of the players suddenly becomes invisible.
The lights go out.
The C.I.A. arrives.
Geoffrey arrives.
One of the players reveals a bomb-shell truth for the first time.

The improvisation continues, but has to include the impact of the third element arriving in the space. The variations are endless and can involve several players, if one wants e.g. the 'knock on the door' could announce the entrance of another player, who is playing 'mother'. And, just imagine, the whole thing started from nothing!

60 SECOND DEATH: I discovered this game in *House of Games*, a drama games book written by Chris Johnston (republished in 2005). It is a great way to invite unpredictable, shadowy, taboo, but potentially comic themes into the Playground. This game requires imaginative courage and conviction to play well.

Two players improvise a scene, which lasts exactly 60 seconds and in which one or both of them die. As with the previous game, they both start off with absolutely no preconception of what might happen. Using the technique of evolving ideas (accepting and rejecting) they very *quickly* find out who they are, where they are, what they are doing and why ... until one of them dies. Anything can happen and the story line very often changes dramatically several times with the 60 seconds of play time. The players are given warnings of how much time they have left ... 30 seconds ... 15 seconds ... five seconds etc.

Note: The scene must continue/last for exactly 60 seconds!

FANTASY LANGUAGE

Speaking Fantasy Language is a technique that professional actors sometimes play with. They might, for example, explore their motivational understanding of written texts by trying to say the whole thing in 'jibberish'. Imagine saying Hamlet's monologue 'To be, or not to be ... ' in a fantasy language. By doing this, the actor reveals how well s/he understands what it is s/he is actually trying to communicate through voice, tone, gesture, emotion and body language alone.

In the Playground, the ability to speak fantasy language serves many purposes, the most important being that when logical words are removed, then the possibility of analytical, intellectual cleverness and witty, verbal dexterity is also removed. Something else has to take its place. And that is usually a far more vibrant and outgoing non-verbal or physical expression of feelings and emotions. The voice increases in agility and range, as do the gestures, in order to reach out for new forms of emotional expression and new ways to achieve one's goals. Non-actors can, through this technique, find a whole new range of ways to express themselves, which is very satisfying for them and an absolute joy to observe. Fantasy language is another brilliant device to de-mechanise habits, overcome blocks and 'stretch' what we call the Actor's Instrument.

An excellent warm up for the following Fantasy Language games would of course be *Body Instruments or Emotional Symphonies* (both already described in *Games – Part 2: Imagination/Mind/Body Games*).

TELL ME A SECRET: I introduce the skill of talking rubbish, by asking one of the players to tell me a secret in fantasy language. If they don't understand what I mean, I demonstrate. I encourage them all, in turn, to tell me a secret, by babbling away at them, in some peculiar version of a language that doesn't exist at all, and then responding to their fantasy language secrets (which no-one really understands) as if I *totally* understand and am truly shocked or amazed at what they have told me! If it goes well, the whole group is inspired to contribute more nonsensical comments and the whole thing becomes a group confessional in double dutch.

I might suggest ways (in English!) in which they could speak the language better through exaggerated articulation of vowels and consonants, but as soon as they are all fairly confident, I introduce the Fantasy Language games, which are ridiculous fun.

FANTASY LANGUAGE CONVERSATIONS: On the stage area, I place three chairs close together, all facing the audience, to create the proverbial park bench.

The game starts off with two players (A + B). A sits on the park bench with his/her eyes closed. B enters the scene, also with his/her eyes closed. The two players begin to have a conversation. Both players should try to keep their eyes closed throughout the improvisation, but not try to act as if they are 'blind people'. They should act and react as if they can see. They should also both speak in Fantasy Language of course, and act as if they totally understand what each other is saying.

The conversation can go anywhere in emotionality and content. Because the logical mind is switched off and the senses are switched on, the players tend to inspire each other and egg each other on in new ways. What starts as a polite, quiet, sensitive scene more often than not ends up in absurd extremes of passion and emotion. The absence of the option of clever, witty verbal negotiations and comic banter is replaced by very unusual facial expressions, vocal agility, weird sounds and a highly charged physical urge to communicate with emotions and feelings, touch and reassurance, plus a heightened listening with alerted senses. The type of conversations I have witnessed have included some or all of the following, most of which are very animated: *polite exchanges; declarations of friendship; outraged arguments; bitter complaints; compassionate shows of sympathy, affection and tenderness; reciprocal flirts; mistaken identities and intentions; absurd elucidations; daft rough and tumbles; wild songs; rhythmical drumming and raunchy dances.*

Things become even more dramatic when I send in a third player (C) to join them, also with eyes closed and speaking Fantasy Language. That's when we start witnessing: *displays of jealousy; curious pauses and tensions; desperate reprisals; stubborn silences; love declarations; animal imitations; group embraces; physical pile ups; ceremonial chanting and war dances.*

The most miraculous thing about this game is that no-one ever gets hurt! 'Blindness' awakens all the *other senses*, in particular *listening, feeling* and *spatial awareness*. The players become *tuned into each other* in a very different way. And because they've got their eyes closed they seem to forget what they look like! The audience watching, of course, is often reduced to tears laughing.

Note: There are many variations of games using fantasy language, but I will only include two more very brief descriptions, in order to inspire some ideas.

FANTASY LANGUAGE IMPROS: I invite two or more players to improvise a scene in fantasy language, but this time they have their eyes open! They are given the situation and setting before they begin e.g.

Robbing a bank and it all goes horribly wrong.
Trying to put up a tent in a very strong wind.
Driving a car down a country lane at night. They are lost and suddenly a vampire appears.

STOP/START FANTASY LANGUAGE: Again two players improvise a scene in fantasy language with their eyes open, but this time, I explain that when I blow a whistle they should immediately switch to normal English (while continuing the conversation, of course). When the whistle blows again they should revert back to fantasy language. This happens several time in the course of the improv-isation. The situation and setting is given before they begin e.g.

> A job interview (one is the interviewer, the other is the interviewee).
> Buying a list of groceries in a shop (one is the shop keeper, the other is the customer).
> A blind date (the couple meet for the first time in a restaurant).

MEMORY GAMES

One thing the players often ask me, as a professional actor, is: 'How do you remember all those lines?' My answer is that for some it's hard work and for others it's a piece of cake. We are all wired differently. For me, it has always been a struggle and to be honest, it takes me ages and a lot of hard work to absorb a large role, to get it under the belt as it were, to learn it off-by-heart to the point that I can say it in my sleep, which is literally what I do! But I've noticed that it does actually get easier the more I do it. One can develop effective *pegging systems*. New neural pathways and synapses in the brain grow to facilitate the storage of new information.

Another thing I've noticed from teaching memory techniques is that, because we are all wired differently, everyone has different types of pegging systems that they quite naturally use ... their own *preferred* systems. Never the less, one can develop more pegging systems if one wants to and layer them. The brain doesn't have to stop developing.

The next game is a fantastic way to show the players how all this can work.

SURREAL POEMS: This challenge is similar to *Abstract Madness* (explained next in this games section under the title *Advanced De-mechanisation*) because it can actually serve many purposes. The most obvious purpose is, of course, to show people that they can actually memorise, prepare and perform things relatively quickly and easily, if they know how. But, within that challenge are embedded multi-skills. I'll explain it in stages:

Stage 1. All participants take a pen and an A4 sheet of paper. At the very top of the paper they write *the first line of a poem*. It can be a poem they know, but even better, a made up poem, which is either beautiful, abstract, silly, mundane, witty, weird, melancholic, surreal, epic, romantic, dark, insane ... whatever ... but just the first line! They then fold that top bit of paper over, so the line they have written is hidden from view. They hand the paper on to the player on their left. Then they all write the second line of a poem (either a continuation of the same poem or a new poem, it doesn't matter), fold it over and hand it on again. They repeat this action *six times in total*. After they have handed it on for the last time, they keep the paper they now have, open it and read it. They now have a *surreal six line poem* that either makes no sense at all, or oddly enough, makes a lot of sense in some weird way. Clearly it will not necessarily rhyme!

Stage 2. I invite the players to learn their poems off by heart in ten minutes or less. They will then be invited to perform it to the rest of the group without the aid of the paper. They all (in their own bubbles) actively rehearse, plan, memorise and design how they will perform their poems. When they have finished preparing, they perform individually in front of the group and then we discuss the results.

Note: It usually only takes them about 5-10 minutes maximum to learn and design their performances, which end up being quite physical, dramatic, intense and entertaining in a delightful '*Alice Through The Looking Glass*' sort of way.

Here are some examples of surreal poems that were written by the players in one of the sessions. Remember that each line was written by a different player, without knowing or seeing what came before:

Throw down your Self on the floor
Did I think you would walk away from me?
It's an up-side-down world, you know
The light blinded me and I fell
Where are all the magicians hiding?
Wondering where all the daffodils went.

Never in a million life-times
Hanging from a weeping willow
No-one could have guessed it
Where are all the magic nights?
The grass is greener, but the cows smell worse
The blossom of my life needed much manure.

The magnificent bird was flying
Crocodiles with the measles
My chest explained to me why my heart was blue
Ingested a tulip, coughed a little
My inner fire is burning ... burning!
Praise the Lord and die, die, die.

Wriggling chocolate covered nuts
The stars of heaven are out tonight
It's all a crazy madcap game
Several ambulances screamed towards the cliff
Nobody recognised the pigmy
And the river, oh the river, it was so blue.

PEGGING SYSTEMS: Before they start to memorise their poems, I always explain something about the different memorisation methods the players can utilise.

There are many different ways to commit lines to memory. *Frequent and fast repetition* is the most common ... and this is particularly effective if you do this *before you go to sleep at night!* But there are many other ways that are less commonly known. So many, I can't possibly list them all here. I tend to describe what, in my opinion, are the four most important pegging systems that seem to be most effective for the majority of people: *Emotional Content; Visual Story Boarding; Physical Anchoring; Spatial Anchoring:*

Emotional Content: The player finds one, or even two lines in their poem that make sense to them *emotionally*. By that I mean a line that pulls at their heart strings; that strikes an emotional chord; something they *personally* can connect with. The player then uses that line (or lines) as a hook or peg to hang the context of the whole poem onto i.e. to justify the other lines and to develop a possible *emotional through-line* or story-line for all the lines. If something *means* something to us on a deeper level then we tend to remember it!

Visual Story Boarding: Visual pegging is probably the most ancient way known by humans to store memory. Aligned with the emotional through-line, the players can begin mapping out the images of a story (if they have not already started doing this). For example, the player can turn each line of the poem into the stages of a rather surreal visual story or dream that they see unfolding. It is easier to remember the step-by-step interconnected stages of a whole story than to remember randomly disconnected items. They can imagine the images taking shape in front of them, as if on a film screen and seen from a distance in a *dissociated* state. But here we have something very interesting. The player can also jump inside the picture and experience the story going on all around them in a 4D *associated* state. An imaginary virtual world, as it were! In the latter state they might be more immersed 'in it' emotionally and physically.

Physical Anchoring: The more engaged physically (and emotionally) the player can be in the rehearsing of the poem's storyline, the better the text will stick in the body, mind, voice and memory. I encourage the players to get up and rehearse it *actively and vocally out loud* i.e. don't sit on your butt and learn with silent mental repetition in a corner somewhere. Get up and experimentally play with 100% commitment physically and emotionally from the outset! In this way all the muscles of the body begin to anchor (store) the memories immediately.

Spatial Anchoring: The player should try to use the *whole stage area*, designating a different space for each line (or stage of the story). This acts like a chorographical peg for the memory i.e. in this space I do, see, hear and feel this ... in that space I do, see, hear and feel that.

Note: These concepts and ideas need to be tried out in order to really appreciate their effectiveness. But I hope the reader gets some idea of the potential of this memory game and will be able to see how the pegging systems can be creatively linked with the players' unique design and performance style of their given Surreal Poem in multi-dimensional ways.

ADVANCED DE-MECHANISATION

I am going to finish this games section (which focused on the quickening, expansion and powerful use of the IMAGINATION) with the description of another de-mechanisation game that I invented called *Abstract Madness*. It engages all the senses, the whole instrument, plus an absurdly heightened imagination ... but, it can also be played whenever there is a need to shake off tensions, have a laugh, loosen up and go beyond the Mask of fear or pretence.

Thus, layer by layer, I enable the players to break through walls of doubt, lose the shoulds and shouldn'ts of the 'real' world and relax deeper into the zone of the *Underbelly*, where we get closer to the essential core self, authenticity and the heart of real confidence. Thus, *Abstract Madness*, with its manifold-purposes, will lead us beautifully into the next games section (*Part 3: Transformation & Truth*).

ABSTRACT MADNESS: This multifaceted imaginative challenge (which revisits some of the techniques described in the *Surreal Poems* challenge) has provided an endless source of amusement for my players (both to play and to watch) for about 30 years and is a fantastic way to introduce several key improvisation/acting skills in one crazy game. It's rather complex and therefore needs to be described carefully in three stages:

Stage 1: The players are all given an A4 sheet of paper and a pen. Each player first writes down three random words e.g. *rubber, blue-bottle, spaghetti ... or ... mouth, duck, perfume ... or ... zenith, magnet, wig*. They then fold the paper over so that the words don't show anymore and hand their piece of paper on to the player on the left. All the players then write down three strong emotions e.g. *furious, hysterically happy, blissful ... or ... miserably morose, panic stricken, totally in love*. Again they fold the paper over and hand it on. This time the players write down three strange things that a human could do e.g. *rolling around in mud; feeding bananas to a crocodile; flying in eternal circles ... or ... swimming in champagne; walking barefoot on broken glass; killing hundreds of cockroaches*. The players then hand the paper onto the next player, who keeps it.

Stage 2: The players get into pairs. Each pair is now invited to create three scenarios that they can perform in a repetitive way. Each scenario is inspired by what they have on their combined two pieces of paper i.e. each pair now has a total of six random words, six strong emotions and six strange actions between them. Each scenario should be inspired by one word, one emotion and one action i.e. they don't use all the suggestions; they mix and match. Using the above examples, I will now put three scenarios together to demonstrate what I mean, although the combinations could be very different:

1.   Panic stricken, they could both be flying in eternal circles, while repeating the word 'blue-bottle.'

2.   They could be walking barefoot on glass, blissfully repeating the word 'rubber'.

3.   They could repeat the word 'mouth', while furiously feeding bananas to a crocodile.

Stage 3: Once they have decided which combinations they like best, I invite each pair to perform their three scenarios in the stage area, in front of the rest of the group. I give them about 5-10 minutes to prepare!

When they are ready, each pair in turn performs their three scenarios 1, 2 and 3, one after the other in sequence, but with the sound of a gong (or whistle) to indicate when they move from one scenario to the next. Yes. This is absurd.

The two players start by bowing very seriously to the audience (the rest of the group) and then to each other in reverential Japanese style. On the sound of the first gong they launch into the first scenario and keep doing it, repeating it and exploring it, in all its extreme variations, until they hear the sound of the second gong. They then launch into the second scenario, exploring and discovering how far they can go with that. At the sound of the third gong they progress to the final scenario (but they are not finished yet!) ... with the sound of the fourth gong, they go back to the first scenario ... and then the second again ... and so on and so forth. The gaps between the gongs and the rate of switches between the scenarios speeds up, going round and round in mad circles, until the players forget what they are doing or are almost merging all three!

Note: This game deserves a more thorough explanation i.e. what on earth's the point of it?!

- **Immersion:** The players learn very quickly to immerse themselves in what they are doing. They learn this by watching. They see what works best and there is no doubt that when the two players on stage really go for it, immersing themselves 'in it' without self-consciously worrying what they look like, really playing together in their own imaginative bubble, supporting each other and focusing on the ridiculous tasks at hand e.g. saying 'mouth' and furiously feeding bananas to a crocodile ... then the whole thing takes off.

- **Out-of-the-Box Inventiveness:** There is something deliciously satisfying about *putting opposite things together* and seeing how they create new dramatic dynamics of invention. Each scenario has its own quality or atmosphere, with different speeds, movements and usages of space e.g. the 1st scenario might be fast and agitated, using the whole space in circles. The 2nd scenario would perhaps be slow, meditative, tense and careful, using only a small amount of space. The 3rd scenario could be a repetitive, manic and jerky backwards and forwards in one direction.

- **Seeing ahead and self-awareness:** The players have to be totally immersed in what they are doing, but also prepared to switch to the next scenario at any unpredictable moment ... multi-tasking, as it were, while watching from 'outside ' of themselves. This creative challenge can be useful as example of *self-awareness* (as mentioned in *Chapter 4 –The Mirror /Self-Awareness*), the paradox being that through this game the players become *less self-conscious* in a shy, inhibited way and more self-aware in an expansive creative way.

Abstract Madness is just another one of those games that needs to be seen to be believed!

So far, we have warmed up, de-mechanised and only just begun to test the landscape of our imaginative freedom. We have perhaps discovered a few blocks that prevent us from engaging with what we truly feel and believe we are capable of. Let us now move on to the next chapter and explore a whole new level of understanding of the power of acting.

THE GAMES
Part 3: TRANSFORMATION AND TRUTH

IN THIS SECTION, we are going to slow right down in order to immerse ourselves much more deeply, and more seriously perhaps, in our inner world of imagination; this vast unexplored terrain that we hardly give the time of day, where we meet the intimately personal and the transpersonal in an archetypical dream realm behind and beyond the Mask.

We'll be looking at concepts and techniques that professional actors use to explore transformation e.g. the *Creative Gaze; The Mask; Body Language; High/Low Status; and Subtext*. As we engage with these creative challenges that help us develop a trusting relationship with our *inner intuitive feelings* and *authenticity*, we will notice how 'acting' becomes less and less about a façade. Paradoxically, it becomes more and more about a search for personal truth.

The following ideas and games are fascinating and revelatory in themselves, but are also intended to prepare the ground for the even more challenging self-discoveries that the players may encounter in the final games section – *Part 4: The Underbelly*.

SLOWING DOWN

In all the years that I have encouraged adults to play, there is one technique that is perhaps more valuable than all of them put together. *Slowing down*.

In the 'real world', adults often feel that they have to *do a lot fast* in order to *achieve a lot*. On stage, adult non-actors may also feel they have do it all *quickly* in order to 'not be boring'. Strangely, in both cases, the opposite is achieved. Speed is almost like a dis-ease, a restlessness that gets us nowhere. Certainly on stage, if you don't slow down and immerse yourself imaginatively in what you are doing, the audience will not have the time or inclination to immerse themselves in what you are doing either. They will simply witness you being stressed.

By slowing down, we awaken our intuitive feelings ... we connect with a different perception of reality ... we give ourselves *time* to go into the inner world, to space out, imagine, see, feel and dream. In this way we reach the desired destination quicker. It comes to us. When we do this on stage, we allow the observer (the audience) to dream too... to dream with us ... to see things in the spaces in between things. In this way, the audience is drawn in. The observer comes to us and with us.

Sometimes it is simply enough to do nothing. The audience, the observer, reads whatever they want into the pauses. The manifestation of creativity is a meeting place somewhere between the observed and the observer. We have to slow down, engage with our own inner truth and let it happen.

> **The more we are able to sustain a strong bond of concentration with visible and invisible objects to which we direct our attention, the closer we will approach an understanding of the nature of real imagination.**
>
> Michael Chekhov 1991:12

THE PRINCESS AND THE POTATOES: This creative visualisation (and the ones that follow in *Stepping Into the Picture* and *Precious Objects*) is an excellent way of demonstrating to beginners how 'the way we see things' transforms us.

I ask the players all to be a Princess, Prince, King or Queen, whichever suits them best. (I have male players who are dying to be a queen and women who want to be kings). In whatever role they choose, I ask them to imagine that they are digging potatoes in a field. Each player finds their own little space in the room and, everyone at the same time, begins to act out the role and the task.

I observe them doing this for a while ... maybe for about 2-3 minutes.

It is clear, on this first attempt at 'pretending to be' someone else, they are all going about it in a rather logical, clichéd and mechanical sort of way. The majority create caricatures from a Pantomime. Great fun, but there is much more to be discovered than that, because it is also clear from their body language and eyes, that they are feeling insecure, checking to see what the others are doing and seeking approval. They are not 'in it'. Some, however, really do get 'into it' in a wonderfully *exaggerated* sort of way, but we are still searching for something else.

After a short while, I ask them to stop and we have a brief discussion about how that felt. The majority say they felt awkward and a bit stupid ... that they couldn't relate to a King or a Princess digging potatoes. I invite them to do it again, but this time, I explain that I will be asking them a series of questions and I want them to observe what comes up for them imaginatively in response to those questions. They need to slow down and pay attention to as much imaginative detail as possible. As follows:

What time of day is it?

What's the weather like?

What year is it?

What are you wearing?

Why are you there?

Is there anyone else with you?

What sounds do you hear?

What's the earth like?

What do your hands look and feel like?

What do the potatoes look and feel like?

How many have you dug up so far?

What were you doing yesterday?

When did you last make love with someone?

What do you have with you?

A bag? What's in your bag?

What's your name?

Where are you going after this?

What are the surroundings like?

Are you hungry?

What do you *want* to do?

What are you feeling right now?

I leave plenty of time between each question so that the players can really get into what they are seeing, feeling, hearing, sensing and doing. There are many more questions I could and sometimes do ask, with embellishments and suggestions, like: 'Can you feel the wind?', 'What does the sky look like?', 'Are there any birds flying over?', 'Are you married or engaged?', 'Do you have any children?', 'Where are they now?'

The second time around, there is a completely different type of atmosphere in the room, a dramatic tension, a spell, an emotional presence. The players are completely absorbed in their own worlds, not 'consciously' noticing what the others are doing. A transformation occurs. They are immersed in the drama, the sensual feelings, the emotions and the story that is unfolding. They are now beginning to *act* with real emotion, conviction and authenticity. They are literally becoming different characters, different beings.

Afterwards, we all sit in a circle and discuss how that felt. We listen to each other's stories. Each story is very different and says a lot about the individual player, about their inner world, what historical or futuristic age they feel attracted to and the potential characters or *archetypes* they intuitively relate to.

Note: As facilitator, I find this creative challenge helps me gain a deeper insight into the unique qualities of each individual player ... about a subconscious yearning that is going on behind the *habitual mask*. For the players too, this represents a major paradigm shift. Here we begin to understand the *transpersonal* power of intuitive imagination. The power of acting.

> **Man feels himself younger and younger, the more he enters into the world of the imagination. He knows that it was only the intellect that made him stiff and aged in his soul expression.**
>
> Rudolf Meyer, excerpt from Michael Chekhov's book 1991:1

STEPPING INTO THE PICTURE: This creative visualisation can be introduced whenever the facilitator feels it would enhance one or more players' understanding of themselves and their unique potential (I refer back to the case study of *Michelle* in *Chapter 4 – The Mirror/The Power of the Mask*, where I first referred to this technique).

I invite all the players in a quiet and reflective moment to slow right down, to sit still with their eyes closed and see a portrait of their dreamed or visionary SELF in their mind's eye. I ask them the following questions and invite them to watch out for details as they emerge. I give them plenty of time to *notice the details* in between the questions:

> Where are you?
> What are you wearing?
> Are you seated? Standing? Lying?
> What era is your portrait painted in?
> Are you inside or outside?
> What is around you?
> Are you alone? Who is with you? Any animals? Objects?
> What colours do you see?
> Are you holding anything? What is it?
> What is your face in the portrait expressing?
> What are your eyes saying or seeing?
> What is the frame of the painting like?
> How big is the portrait?
> Can you see anything unexpected?

I then invite them all to *step into the portrait* and *become that vision of themselves*. I ask them to *notice what it feels like*. I note the changes and transformations in the players' facial expressions and physical presence; their posture, their breath. I allow them to remain in those 'personas' for a little while, move about a bit and look around them. This doesn't have to take long. Just a few moments.

Afterwards, they return to the room again, into 'normality' and a discussion ensues about what the individual unique portraits looked like and how the players were affected physically and emotionally by becoming that version of their SELF.

Note for the discussion: Michael Chekhov explored how the imagined image can take on a life of its own.

> **The images pass through two phases: the first, in which they are directly influenced by your creative "gaze", and the second, in which they develop independently with your assistance**
>
> Chekhov 1991:13

PRECIOUS OBJECTS: This creative visualisation demonstrates yet another way of entering an alternative character. It has already been briefly described in the context of a case study involving a potato, a rag doll and a cliff edge! (see *Chapter 4 – The Mirror/Being Dangerous*). Using their imagination the players develop a character's name, history and life mission via a dreamed up relationship with a chosen object.

I bring a basket full of objects to the session ... things that I find in junk shops or around the house which have some kind of symbolic meaning e.g. *A conch shell. A knife. A box. A large stick. A white or red veil. A key. A child's toy. A pair of sunglasses. A clove of garlic. A leather pouch. A mirror. An empty note-book and pen. A potato. A hat. A rope. A stone. A tin of sardines. A brooch. A feather. A large black drape. A handkerchief. A wooden spoon. A watch that has stopped ... and so forth.*

Stage 1: The objects are placed on the floor and the players choose the object that they wish to play with. They take their time to choose something that intuitively inspires them or they can personally connect to in some way.

Stage 2: I invite the players to get to know their object really well, explaining that they will later create an improvisation with it and that they need to imagine that it is very precious to them. I ask them questions, which will help them evolve their relationship with their chosen object.

> How long have you had it?
> Where did you find it or how did it come to you?
> Why is it so important to you?
> Why do you always carry it with you?
> Where do you hide it normally? Or why do you keep it on your person?

Who are you?
Where are you going?
Where have you come from?
What would happen if you lost it or if it was stolen or destroyed?
What do you want out of life?

Stage 3: Intuitively, without knowing the stories that the players have formed in their minds, I invite two of them to meet on stage in a given meeting place i.e. a setting that has been randomly chosen by me with (perhaps) no knowledge of who they are or what will happen e.g.

At a cross-road on the moors.
On a cliff edge.
In another dimension.
In the middle of a jungle.
In a striptease club at three o'clock in the morning.
In a medieval tavern.
In a prison cell.
In the middle of a forest on a full moon night.

The players meet in the stage area and through the technique of 'advancing ideas' the development of a story, a relationship, a drama evolves out of the precious objects (as described in the case study of the players on the *cliff edge* with the *ragdoll* and the *potato*).

Note: These rather surreal improvisations function best when the players are encouraged to develop a new acting technique. LISTENING. They have to *actively listen to each other;* ask questions and get to know each other. They have to *generously give each other space and time* in order to open up and reveal things that make the improvisation interesting to watch. In short, the players should not 'hog' the drama for them self! The audience wants to know about both characters and delights in the relationship that can develop between the characters. Generous listening skills are absolutely essential if any improvised scene is to evolve to new levels!

LISTENING AND CONFIDENCE

Here begins a fascinating discussion, which can be revisited time and time again throughout the Playground process, because of the depth and breadth of the insights gained and their value in so many different contexts, both on stage and off.

Before I can describe more games, let us explore this subject in order to provide the reader/player with a few thoughts to reflect on.

WHAT IS REAL LISTENING? Listening is very much about hearing the words that people speak, but real listening is so much more than that. It is a whole body sensory experience. For this, we have to slow right down and be still. If you are nervous and hectic, you won't be able to really listen. We are talking about the ability to be silent, at least for a moment, to breathe with the person one is listening to, to tune into their wavelength, witness and empathise. This does not have to take long. Empathic energy travels at the speed of light. Nor does one have to lose a sense of Self. But one does have to slow down.

My experiences in professional acting and teaching have shown me that this skill actually requires *Self-assurance* and *confidence*.

So, let us take an in depth look at this supremely important aspect of acting, on which the development of all of the techniques mentioned so far are utterly dependent ... CONFIDENCE ... surely related to the verb: *to confide*.

WHAT IS CONFIDENCE OR LACK OF IT? This is a very interesting question, which I ask the players to meditate on and share thoughts about, before I reveal what I personally have learnt and know through acting.

On stage, the physical and mental embodiment of confidence is sometimes called *High Status*. The status I am talking about hasn't necessarily got anything to do with *rank*. A King doesn't always feel confident. A tramp may well feel he is King of the Castle. Confidence is as much about conscious 'ownership' of *space and time and choice*, as it is about a given title or rank. It's about being the response-able owner of who you are and what you do. More than anything else, it is about self-awareness and self-belief. This is what gives one the assurance and ability to be confidently silent, to trust your self and others, to listen and generously give other people space and time, without feeling one is losing importance or presence.

A trained actor has to become very familiar with the state of *high confidence*, physically, mentally, emotionally (and spiritually, I believe) not with the intention of necessarily dominating. Saying that, confidence certainly does give one the ability to be actively engaging and convincingly authoritarian! This is a vital part of an actor's ability to *hold the audience's attention, to mesmerise* ... but this 'talent' includes the ability to be *powerfully silent, attentive, to listen, to be compassionate and to be still*. To do nothing.

We are not taught about how to feel truly confident in school. We are not given an inkling of these skills ... even though this knowledge is intimately entwined with one's self-belief and therefore also the effectivity of creative learning. The development of assertiveness (which is not what real confidence is about) seems to be left to children to explore for themselves in the school playground, where the 'reality' is often cruelly competitive. That appears to be one of the foundation stones of learning in the Western capitalist world; to adapt quickly, smartly and assertively to a ferociously competitive world, with a reward system that promotes compliance with a power system.

It isn't surprising that the majority of the adult players arrive in the Playground with a very good understanding of what it is to feel *low status* and full of self-doubt. This lack of confidence can manifest in a variety of ways, accompanied by nervous habits of saying and doing too much or not daring to say anything at all. Some have inflexible, defensive boundaries that let nothing and nobody in. Others may have a tendency to take up as *little space as possible* with seemingly *no* defensive boundaries what so ever.

In contrast, a few players in my sessions, are actually quite good at playing *high status*. They have 'adapted well' to the outside world. They take up an enormous amount of space and refuse to back down! In the Playground they need to learn the invaluable skill of backing off and … generously giving others space to play. Some literally have to re-discover how to feel *vulnerable*. Feeling low status is a state some people don't willingly want to go to. It worries them. It reminds them of unpleasant things. It makes them feel that they will lose everything if they lose their Mask of confidence. This is not true confidence.

Either way, for the majority of the participants, exploring real CONFIDENCE and real LISTENING SKILLS gives rise to many of those enlightening 'Aha' moments; fascinating discoveries, pervaded with deep human insights and paradoxical contradictions.

Before I explain further, it's important that we are all talking about the same thing when referring to 'status'. To reiterate, status, in a drama context, does not describe 'social rank', although it is also that. It is more about the individual's *perception* of who they are and how they *feel* in relation to the people they encounter. It is a question of *relativity* and *context*. People might feel high status in one context and low status in another. We can feel confident in the presence of some people, but not in the presence of others. And there are other variables that need to be discussed: *Inner motivations (are we driven by fear or love)* and *Cultural/social perceptions*.

- **Inner Motivations:** A Guru/Buddha is greatly respected and perceived as high status in a generous and benignly authoritative way. S/he takes up an enormous amount of space with his/her aura and presence, which is said to be keenly felt and observed by his devotees for miles around. A Tyrant also takes up an enormous amount of space, but usually by claiming territory with barbed wire, iron walls, armies to protect him/her and guarded boundaries. The latter attempts to rule the world through rigid control and gains respect through intimidation and fear. The former through connection with some kind of higher consciousness and the power of love. Both can be perceived as, and are often felt as, *high status*. In a similar way, we can observe both positive and negative aspects to *low status* e.g. a humble Samaritan or a scheming wretch. Both appear to be defined by the person's *inner intension* or *life motivation* ... what they are attempting to achieve, how and why.

- **Social Perceptions:** There is also the *outer perception* of society with regard to the contrasting 'roles' of adult and child, teacher and pupil, masculine and feminine. There are moral judgements in place that dictate which members of society are *expected or permitted* to be high status, in control, to display wisdom, authority, knowledge, assertiveness, loudness, boldness or aggression ... in contrast to those members of society who are *expected or permitted* to be low status, lacking in control, wisdom and knowledge, display compassion, purity, submissiveness, simplicity, ignorance or servitude.

After an initial discussion about what confidence might be, seen through the eyes and experiences of the players, I give them a list of contrasting status attributes, which I have assembled over the years. The list (see Fig.1) is in part extracted from Keith Johnstone's book *Impro*, to which I have added my own observations. It functions as inspiration for a further discussion about the various body language characteristics, during the confidence games.

Figure One

High Confidence (High Status)	Low Confidence (Low Status)
Controlled movements	Uncontrolled movements
Keeps head/spine still	Fidgets
No fidgeting	Hands to face and head
Holds eye contact	Can't hold eye contact
Steady gaze	Blinks and twitches

Complete sentences	Umms and eeers ...
Good Posture	Awkward posture
Balanced	Out of balance
Relaxed	Tense
Deep slow breathing	Short high breaths
Smiles with teeth showing	Smiles with top teeth over lower lip
Laughs freely	Giggles
Belly laughter	Forced laughter
Extrovert	Introvert
Open Body	Closed Body
<u>Takes up a lot of space</u>	<u>Takes up as little space as possible</u>
Calculated reactions	Sudden reactions
Planned attacked	Knee jerk reactions
Turns back on people	Watchfully seeks confirmation
Unapologetic	Apologetic
Says very little	Talks too much
Expects or demands service	Willing to please
Unemotional	Emotional
Dark Glasses (to cover the eyes)	Dark Glasses (to cover the eyes)

When we look at some of these physical attributes in relation to our self or the people we encounter in our daily lives or on screen e.g. the boss at work, our parents, our children, our friends, the tyrant in the James Bond movies, the gurus or idols that fascinate us, one can perhaps recognise that the majority of people exhibit a *strange mixture of both weak and strong attributes* with maybe a predominance of a certain kind. There is rarely a stable factor. A famous rock star wearing dark glasses may well have a nervous twitch or the strange habit of scratching his nose or his head. A seemingly shy, reserved child may well sometimes speak in very clear sentences and be able to hold eye contact very well indeed.

We can also observe that there are advantages to be gained from assuming the appearance of both 'confidence' (high status) or 'lack of confidence' (low status).

For example, an important diplomat or aristocrat may, in some situations, be advantaged by playing the role of an approachable, humble personality. A disadvantaged person, may well benefit greatly from assuming the traits of a leader. In almost every situation and individual there is a *tension*, a tug-of-war between the extremes, between opposing aims, motivations and desires ... the moral and the instinctual, the logical and the intuitive, right and wrong, the masculine and the feminine and countless other synergies that co-exist in a fluctuating state of psychic ambition, fear and conflict.

Therefore, *when two people come together* in one space (as in *Precious Objects*, which I have already described, or the *Tension Envelopes* game, which I will describe shortly), a whole range of energies and counter-energies come to the surface, in the exploration of the *relationship* between the two.

The following games are designed to develop the players understanding of the *habitual roles* they tend to choose to play and provide opportunities for them to try out *new roles*; to swop status, to switch the power balance where necessary and discover what real confidence and real power can feel like.

CHANGING STATES: There are typically two approaches that professional actors use to facilitate and precipitate the manifestation of altered states: one is *External* and the other is *Internal*. Combining the two approaches is a very effective way to change state, because there is a two way impact that inevitably causes them to reinforce each other.

1. THE EXTERNAL APPROACH – For this, one starts by imitating the physical qualities of a desired state via the Mask i.e. the external appearance, body language, gestures, shape of the spine, posture, eyes and facial expression ... and then notices how this makes one feel emotionally. For example, the player could try simulating one or two of the High/Low Confidence attributes (listed in fig.1) and see how this makes him/her feel!

2. THE INTERNAL APPROACH – For this, one does the reverse. The player begins by accessing the feelings of the desired state via imagination and/or sensual recall. This is the Stanislavski technique known as *Sense Memory*, which I will be describing in much greater detail later (in *Games – Part 4: The Underbelly/Feeling*). In short, the player is invited to try to remember a time s/he felt either high or low in confidence and then notice the physical impact i.e. the changes that these memories/feelings have on the Mask, the spine, the gestures, the body language etc. **Note:** It may be that some players really struggle *internally* to remember a moment that they felt confident, in which case I suggest they *try imagining something that would make them feel great!*

Extra Note: When I introduce the players to both techniques, I am of course watching carefully out for which players are more comfortable with which approach and in which role ... high status or low status! One can discuss the players' experiences and perceptions, if one wants, before moving on to any of the following games.

STATUS ENCOUNTERS: I set up the proverbial park bench in the centre of the stage area. Two players (A + B) are invited to sit or stand on the stage in whatever way they feel inclined. I ask them both, first to take on the role of Low Status, using both techniques mentioned above, the *internal* and *external*. When they are immersed in the feeling, they should then try to engage in a conversation with each other. The creative challenge is to try to feel/appear *lower status than the other player!* The rest of the group observes and judges which of the two players comes across as lowest in status. Afterwards, the players try the same thing again, but with High Status.

This sounds like a competition. But I assure everyone that this is in no way about who can act best! It is an opportunity to explore, experience and observe how people, consciously or unconsciously, affect each other with their behaviour patterns. It demonstrates how we can develop conscious choice, if we become more aware of the effects we are creating and, of course, it opens up discussions about *Mask, Body-language, Emotions and Feelings*.

The results are fascinating, quite funny and very revealing. Sometimes we think we are doing one thing, but in fact it looks like we are doing the opposite! For example, turning your back on someone, because you're shy or reserved, can look like you're not interested in what the other person is saying. This might make you look higher status than them, when actually you're not feeling that way at all!

It is also interesting to note, how the viewer's *perceptions* of the same thing might differ completely. The way we choose to see or interpret things, depends ultimately on how we feel inside.

Note: After each participant has had a go at the above *same status* conversations, then they can try another variation of the same improvisation, but with *opposing statuses,* where A is high status and B is low status or vice versa. After this they can move onto an even more advanced version involving *swop overs,* where one player starts low status and ends high status, and the other player starts high status and ends low status. This prepares them for the *Power Swop* improvisations, which will be described shortly.

COMIC POWER PLAY: This game provides a comically over-the-top way of exploring the physical and psychic extremes of confidence, dominance, power and/or vulnerability without the stress of negative judgement.

Two players take the stage. One is the *top-dog*. The other, the *under-dog*, has to do whatever the top-dog orders them to do, with one proviso: They both have to speak in fantasy language! The boss has to command the other player around using physical gestures, breath, sounds and fantasy language only! The under-dog tries their best to do what the top-dog wants, but doesn't always understand exactly what s/he means! The top-dog's attempts at articulating commands become more and more absurd, extrovert and inventive. Needless to say, it is very funny and, of course, every player gets the chance to be *the boss* and *the under-dog!*

POWER SWOPS: Things are now heating up in terms of improvisational skills, motivation and the confidence to play with *new roles*. This next game gives the players the opportunity to design and develop more imaginatively complex characters. They are invited to use all or any of the skills and concepts they have already been introduced to e.g. *Advancing Ideas, Slowing Down, Stepping into a Picture, Developing a Relationship with an Object, Status Attributes, Power Play* tactics, *Listening Skills, Generosity* ... but here we are adding something new!

A HIDDEN AGENDA. A SUBTEXT. A SECRET MISSION OR OBJECTIVE.

Every character and personality on stage and in life has an AIM, a GOAL, an OBJECTIVE; something they want (or don't want) to achieve or gain either in life, in a given situation or within a relationship. Usually our life goal is the thing that ultimately drives us. We want our father's love; we want acknowledgement from our mother; we want to prove something; we don't want to be poor etc. Sometimes we know what it is. Other times, we try to get what we want, despite not consciously knowing what it is we want (or don't want)!

In this particular challenge it is the servant who has a specific objective in mind, in the form of a 'hidden agenda', something they don't at first speak about, but which later in the scene is revealed and which brings about a complete reversal of status in both players!

There are two players (**A** is the master and **B** is the servant):

> **A:** invents a high status character e.g. Boss of a big business; Master/Mistress of a large estate; Gang leader of a gang of criminals etc. At the start of the scene s/he oozes confidence, self-assurance, assertiveness, boldness, economy of movement and speech, and clarity of mind. All the attributes of a seemingly confident person. S/he can appear either benign or malevolent. Either way, s/he takes up and *owns* the whole space. *It is his/her space.*

> **B:** also invents a character, compatible with A's character e.g. the boss' secretary; the masters' servant; a petty thief, who's recently joined the

gang etc. At the start of the scene s/he displays all the attributes of low self-esteem. S/he is grovelling, apologetic, nervous, snivelling and humble, again either appearing good or evil. Either way, s/he *doesn't own the space*. BUT (this is the important bit) ... s/he has a 'hidden agenda'!

The Hidden Agenda should be thought out by B, 'secretly', prior to their entrance. For example, s/he has some evidence of a shocking and humiliating scandal involving A, the Top Dog. S/he is waiting for the right moment to reveal what s/he knows and thereby take advantage of the situation. This is his/her 'trump card', which neither A nor the audience (the rest of the group) knows about. The scandal could be adultery, child abuse, treason, murder, tax evasion, financial corruption, false identity, forgery ... the list is long. The under-dog can have fun thinking up something psychologically clever and really meaty to accuse the top-dog of!

Impro Directions: A calls B into the room, or B knocks, begging for admittance. There is a preliminary interaction, which establishes their relationship. A bosses B around in whatever way they wish (this time in a normal language!) At the right moment, B begins to reveal what s/he knows. A may at first try to deny it, but in the end cannot deny that it is true. The evidence is clear. It is very humiliating for A, who ends up being desperate and apologetic, grovelling if needs be, pleading for mercy, while B assumes higher and higher status, revelling in the act of taking complete control. B can now ask A for anything they want. *B now owns the space!*

Note: It is important that both players have enough time to prepare and *step into their new roles*. Also, I encourage both parties, both at the beginning and the end of the improvisation to really enjoy the dominance! They can relish getting the other to grovel. They do not have to be 'nice'!!! Likewise, in turn, both players have to be able to be *strategically and generously* submissive. The top-dog can't simply deny the accusations. S/he has to admit guilt. And, if B pulls out an imaginary gun, then A will have to generously accept that the gun is loaded and that the other player has the ultimate power and authority. This is an agreement.

I say this because, for those that usually enjoy feelings of confidence, submission can be a challenge. It won't come naturally! Just as it can be a challenge for those who prefer to play low status to exert power and control over others, be it justifiable or not. After a while, they all get the hang of it and thoroughly enjoy this form of 'dramatic' play.

Advanced Versions: As the players develop more subtle skills, they can be challenged to use more and more *authentic* and believable tactics. They can be invited to explore a whole range of situations and roles, some requiring a bigger imaginative stretch than others e.g. Toilet Lady and Aristocrat in a Powder Room; Prisoner and Jailer; Carer and Patient; Car Park Attendant and Car Owner; Head Teacher and Teenage Student; Next Door Neighbours; Boss and Employee; Psychiatrist and Client; Husband and Wife; Parent and Child; Customer and Sales Person; Police and Tramp; Pimp and Whore; Pirate Captain and First Mate; Pope and Priest; Magician and Apprentice etc.

Although some of these improvisations can be set up as 'fun' character/ status explorations, they inevitably also invite the expression of very *real* projected or suppressed feelings. The players are beginning to understand more about the impact of their own personal 'real life' objectives and normally unspoken feelings. The clowning around tends to stop at some point. The dramas become intense, serious and convincing. A discussion about acting, *authenticity* and *truth*, quite naturally ensues.

AUTHENTICITY CHALLENGES

We've now got to a point in the process, where the players are fascinated by what is coming up and being revealed. The imagination is flowing, they understand various key techniques, they know how to immerse themselves in what they are doing, risks are being taken, the whole gestalt being is loosened up, the defences are down and some kind of truth will out. It cannot be prevented anymore.

The suppressed emotional truth wants to be seen, it longs to be heard, it needs to be felt. This is where we can begin to take a more in depth look at some of the skills professional actors explore to deliver *truth and authenticity*. We are ready.

The following two games (*Tension Envelopes; Opposing Truths*) challenge the players to explore the tension of *relationship*, to listen to and watch each other and to express very honest feelings straight from the heart, where appropriate. These games require that the players play with a more focused attention to detail and to feel the impact of their own authentic feelings more intensely.

TENSION ENVELOPES: I explain to all the players that there is an invisible white line that travels around the four edges of the stage, plus two white lines leading diagonally from one corner to the other, forming a cross centre stage (rather like the outlines of an envelope). They are *only permitted to walk on the imaginary white lines*, but are permitted to 'push the envelope' (test the boundaries) in terms of where they take the emotional dynamics of the game.

Two players are asked to stand in opposite corners, simply being themselves, in whatever state they choose to be in, and to *focus their complete attention on each other* (as if the audience doesn't exist). This focus is held best by maintaining as much eye-contact with each other as possible or by sensing the presence of the other player through peripheral vision, which requires *a whole body/sense awareness*. When they are ready they should begin to walk on the lines, exploring and playing with increasing and decreasing distance and tension between each other ... always maintaining this type of intense focus.

Gradually we (the audience) witness a relationship emerging, which is based on the personalities of the two players; the tendencies of their 'habitual person-alities' to either dominate or be submissive, to chase or to run away, to offer playful suggestions or to reject them, to flirt or to be coy, to be serious or silly, to take up a lot of space or to give space to the other.

More often than not it starts in a playful way, which is great, but, after a while, I encourage the players to explore potential gut feelings and intuitive instincts; feelings of threat, fear, menace, attraction, friendship, bonding and/or danger between them. It can develop into anything from a match of wits to an intimate confrontation, a playful run about, a flirt or a full on test of nerves i.e. a very real exploration of likes, dislikes, strengths and weaknesses.

Needless to say, the subtleties of eroticism are played out. How could they not be? The whole of life is an exploration of intimacy, more or less, within the boundaries of what we are told or experience as acceptable. However, it goes hopefully without saying that the crossing of more explicit sexual boundaries should be reserved for private.

All in all, it is fascinating to watch. I don't know a better or faster game to get the players to:

- use as much space as possible
- hold eye contact and intensely focus attention on the other player
- be aware of the degrees of physical and psychic tension caused by proximity
- appreciate the rich pregnancy of silence and stillness ... doing nothing, apart from breathing and feeling

A discussion about how it felt and what was observed naturally ensues.

Advanced Version: Play this with three players and the dynamics are very different. One or all of them in turn invariably end up playing *piggy-in-the-middle* or the *outsider*.

OPPOSING TRUTHS: This challenge can lead directly on from Tension Envelopes, if one so wishes. It is a highly *cathartic* game for adult players who have gained a degree of confidence. I will need to explain it in detail; in perhaps more detail than any of the other games. Along with high/low status, listening and confidence, it deserves a whole chapter of its own!

I developed the idea for *Opposing Truths* from some method acting exercises that I picked up somewhere. I'm not sure where. *Method Acting* evolved in America out of Stanislavski's famous system of teachings about imagination and 'truth'. Playing with method techniques requires an appreciation of authenticity and is a brilliant way of engendering a far greater sense of honesty and intimacy amongst players.

Opposing Truths is a power game in which non-actors discover (perhaps for the first time) what 'acting' is really about. But more than that. Through it, they can discover new ways to manage emotional and upsetting situations in 'real life'; skills they describe as being life-changing. For example, I have seen players find ways to hold their own, against strong attack; become assertive, where they would normally (in 'real life') back down or break down. I have seen some players soften, break down and cry, where they would normally become rigid, aloof and cold. I have seen a beautiful release and warming, in the face of love. I have seen direct honesty in the face of what appear to be lies.

With this creative challenge, we witness the discovery of new forms of self-expression. One player might learn to reach out and demand for the first time, while another player might learn to say NO for the first time ... although, at this stage we are really only just beginning. I would, in fact, highly recommend returning to *Opposing Truths* at regular intervals with fresh perspectives of what's possible, after experiencing some of the later games. The players are always up for playing it, without a doubt, because it is so valuable for everyone who plays and watches.

Opposing Truths rests on the principle that there are always two sides to an argument. It takes two to tango. It is the synergy or tension between the opposites that creates drama on stage, as it does in life. No-one is ever completely right, nor completely wrong. Where there is light, there is always shadow. The opposites may never agree. The differences may never be resolved, but at least the players begin to see and accept that the opposites exist, not in spite of, but because of each other ... and there is some peace to be found in that.

> **Those who would have right without its correlative,
> wrong; or good government without its correlative
> misrule – they do not apprehend the great principles
> of the universe nor the condition to which all creation is
> subject. One might as well talk of the existence of heaven
> without that of earth, or the negative principle without
> the positive, which is absurd. Such people, if they do
> not yield to argument, must be fools or knaves. (Chuang
> Tzu -Taoist) ... The Taoists realized that no single concept**

or value could be considered absolute or superior. If being useful is beneficial, then being useless is also beneficial.

Zweig & Abrams 1991:252

So, the *Opposing Truths* game involves two players (A and B). The two players are asked to focus on each other in a similar way to the last game and to use the whole stage area, but do not need to stick to the invisible lines that were drawn out in Tension Envelopes. Each player is given *only three things that they are permitted to say*, both sets of which represent their opposing truths, for example:

A: 1. You're Lying. 2. Don't touch me. 3. Never.
B: 1. I love you. 2. Trust me. 3. I just want to hold you.

A: 1. I have to go. 2. It's impossible. 3. You're on your own now.
B: 1. Please stay. 2. I need you. 3. What am I going to do without you?

A: 1. You're fired! 2. It's over. 3. That was your last chance.
B: 1. I can change. 2. It wasn't my fault. 3. Give me another chance ... please.

A: 1. You have no idea. 2. It's not what you think. 3. I love him/her.
B: 1. I'm not going to let this happen. 2. Have you gone mad? 3. I said NO!

A: 1. It's always about you! 2. You never listen to me. 3. I'm trying to tell you something.
B: 1. Shut up! 2. I can't take anymore! 3. You're talking complete bullshit!

A: 1. You don't want to know ... 2. Forget it. 3. You're lying.
B: 1. I do want to know ... 2. Tell me. 3. I love you.

The two players (A and B) can repeat their sentences as many times as they want, in any order, but they can only say those three things. They can also say *nothing at all*, if they want, or repeat one sentence many times. The players have to explore the extremes of expression, the whole gamut of feelings, attitudes, persuasive tactics, emotions or lack of them, approaches and responses, in order to get their point across and succeed in convincing the other player of their truth, but with only three sentences!

This is how I would coach them in this game:

- **Personalise the things that you have been given to say.** Make them your own. You need to reach out, through personal *memory or empathy*, to situations where you can remember or imagine those things being said. Don't say anything unless you truly believe it.

- **Pay attention to what you see and hear.** The target is the other player. *Maintain eye contact as much as possible* either directly or with your peripheral, whole body sensory awareness. Really *listen* to what the other player is saying ... *how* they say it. *Watch and feel* how they are behaving. Think of different ways to change their opinion or state. How can *you* change your approach, in order to influence the attitude, intention or feelings of the other player?

- **Pay attention to what you are feeling**. You have to react in a way that is authentic; honestly responsive to what is coming at you, while *remaining true to your own convictions*. How does the other player affect you emotionally? Take it in. Feel it. **Note:** One might ask, how is it possible to pay attention to two things at once? To focus intently on the other and on one's own feelings? We are capable of multi-tasking on many levels all the time. Through learning to act one simply becomes more self-aware and aware of the whole situation at the same time. This is a chance to experience the phenomenon of being a witness to your own actions.

- **Take it to another level.** Where there is an opportunity, I encourage the players to *take the drama up a notch to another level of intensity*, where there is more to be gained or more to lose. Let it become a *life and death challenge* e.g. A: How important is it for you to leave? If you say you have to leave, then why are you still in the room!!!? B: How important is it to make this person stay in the room? Will you die or starve or be killed if s/he leaves?

- **Do nothing.** Don't be afraid of stillness and long tense pauses. It's not a Ping-Pong match i.e., you said that, so I have to say this etc. It is better to do nothing than to react in a false or forced way. Out of the silence emerges something else. **Note:** I write more about *silence* and *stillness* later, as many people are afraid of silence and it is an incredibly important acting technique. And life skill.

- **Touch**. Don't be afraid of touching the other player, both tenderly and strongly (but without hurting!) This game is not just a verbal challenge. It is a physical challenge: "I just want to hold you". But, if you don't want to be touched: "Don't touch me!" – then make sure that person doesn't come anywhere near you! Keep your distance. Why get close, if you don't want them to touch you?! Say NO to touch, if it is threatening or undesired.

  - **Swop roles.** This is a useful way of experiencing what it feels like from the other player's perspective.

Advanced Version: Can this get more advanced? Yes. After the initial exploration of the opposing tensions with just three sentences each, they can begin to improvise a development or resolution to the situation *with the addition of their own words*. This is a test of their personal identification with the words they are saying. What is the story they have been identifying with? How can the conflict of the different stories be resolved? These are very advanced improvisation skills, which can greatly enhance one's ability to resolve conflicts in life.

SUBTEXT

I've mentioned the word subtext a few times now. It's a fascinating acting technique that can again be applied in 'real' life. A visible invisible. It is what is going on behind the Mask of who we present ourselves to be.

I guess in therapeutic or role-play settings we would define SUB-TEXT as 'non-verbal communication'. In theatre it's a bit more than that. It goes deeper. In a written form, it is the text behind the text. It is the *unspoken inner voice* i.e. the things we consciously know, think, want and feel, but don't say. For example, an actor might say audibly: 'I love you' (because it is written in the text), but be thinking: 'I really don't have the time for this.' This is very different from saying: 'I love you', while thinking 'I need you' or 'I want you'.

Subtext is what is not written, or not said, but what colours the spoken word, what gives it an unmistakeably different feel or quality, via the tone, the inflection, the accompanying gesture, the way the body is open or closed or through the glance in the eyes.

An actor may have a whole string of things to say and do, all written into the body of the script or text, but the subtext is what he and the director decide is really going on in the spaces between the words and actions. It needs to be discovered. One could say that the subtext *is more important* than the text itself, as it is always present in the background of the actors mind. It is the continuum.

It fills the silences and the pauses. That is why subtext is a highly treasured technique in the acting business, particularly in film ... because the camera films *what's going on in the mind*. This is a secret acting tip.

Subtext is also very specific. There is a big difference, for example, between thinking: 'I *want* you' and 'I *need* you'. Once decided upon i.e. what the person is really thinking/feeling, what their real *intention, objective, goal* or *motivation* is, what they *really want to get out of life, the situation or the relationship*, then the subtext can be firmly set in the inner mind of the player as an unspoken thought… or mantra that they repeat silently e.g. 'I am so sorry.' 'Please forgive me.' We are talking about the inner workings of the mind; what goes on behind the Mask.

Here are some games I have developed to discover the impact of *subtext*.

INNER VOICES: The group decides what *two roles* they would like to see played out on stage and who is going to play them. I ask them to keep it absolutely simple e.g. two brothers; a husband and wife; two flat mates; neighbours; a boss and an employee; a nurse and a patient; a customer and a sales person; two teenagers; mother and son etc. The group then decides what the situation is, again keeping it as simple as possible i.e. *where they are, what time of day it is, what they are both doing together.* For example, the husband (A) and wife (B) might be eating breakfast at home or the boss has invited the employee into his office to discuss something important. The two chosen players are then both *separately* and *secretly* given their subtexts.

As an example, let us take the scenario with the husband and wife at breakfast.

> **A's subtext could be:** 'I'm so sorry.' OR it could be: 'Please forgive me'.
> **B's subtext could be:** 'I'm furious with you.' OR it could be: 'Don't come near me'.

It is not necessary for A or B to know exactly *why* they are either furious or sorry (although they could, if they wanted to, personalise it). The two players are simply asked *never* to speak the subtext out loud, but to repeat it over and over again as a silent 'inner mantra' or like an *inner voice* that they tune into as often as possible.

At the same time they should attempt to carry on a normal conversation. 'Do you want some more coffee?', 'Shall I cook supper tonight?', 'What about the parent's evening tomorrow?', 'Aren't you going to be late for work?', 'Sorry, what did you say?', 'It's lovely weather today.', 'You've burnt the toast.' ... whatever. If they keep thinking and repeating their subtext silently, even in the pauses and silences, the whole scene will be filled with a tension that hinges on the expression in their eyes, the inflection and tone of their voices, their movements, the way they pick things up or put things down, the way they are seated in relation to each other, the way they breath, walk and talk.

Note: The other players watch out for the impact and try to guess what the subtext of both players is. There is endless room for experimentation, exploration and discussion with this game, asking what works best and what is most effective. Studying and playing with *subtext* makes the player much more conscious of the *subtleties of body-language*, both his/her own and those of others.

Advanced Note: Combined with the Mask technique (as described in *Chapter 2 – The Mirror/The Power of the Mask/Fixed Facial Expressions*) the Inner Voice technique can radically change the way one feels in 'real' life. Try smiling all day and saying repeatedly, as an inner mantra, 'Life is so exciting!' It could work wonders on the spirit. Certainly it will make a difference.

SECRET MISSIONS: This is a game I invented a long time ago and have gradually developed to its current form. It is based on the idea that each player has a mission to get something out of or from the other player, or to get them to do something. It requires all the skills that the players have been introduced to so far, but this time, more than anything else, I encourage the players to focus on *listening* and *being generous*; giving each other time and space to get what they want. In fact, the trick is to find out what the other player's mission is and *support* him/her in achieving it ... while using the information gathered as a potential means of achieving one's own mission!

Two players (A and B). The group decides what roles they are going to play, where they are and what they are doing ... but not *why*. Again, I ask everyone to keep it very simple e.g. a boyfriend and girlfriend, who've known each other for one year and who are having a meal in a restaurant; two friends, who are moving into a flat together for the first time; husband and wife on their annual holiday in Mallorca; two brothers taking a Sunday walk along a cliff path; two sisters sharing Christmas together alone. Nothing more needs to be said.

The two chosen players think up a *secret mission* (or are given one, either by myself or one of the other players) i.e. something they want to achieve in this situation with regard to the other player. As an example, let us take the two brothers walking on the cliff path:

> **Brother A's** secret mission is to persuade his brother to lend him £5,000 to repay a gambling debt.

> **Brother B's** secret mission is to confess to his brother that he has had a long term love affair with his (A's) wife.

At the start of the improvisation, the two players have no idea what the other wants, plans or expects. (The majority of the viewers don't know either!) In the example above, the potential outcome for both is fairly straight forward: Brother A uses Brother B's guilt as a motive for persuasion and brother B is happy to oblige. However, the missions are not always that straightforward or complimentary and things can turn out quite differently. For example, what if?:

> **Brother A's** secret mission is to tell his brother that he (A) has a limited time to live and wants to invite his brother on a world cruise.
>
> **Brother B's** secret mission is to tell his brother that he has had a long term love affair with his (A's) wife and that they are planning to go away and live abroad together.

In this second scenario there is a real conflict. How will they both achieve their goals and resolve this? Will all three go on a cruise together? Or, will one brother end up pushing the other brother over the cliff edge!? I encourage the players to take their time. *Don't be afraid of pauses.* Use the weather and the spectacular sea view, for example, to immerse yourself in the situation and give yourself time to adjust to what is coming at you. Silence is golden. Don't give away your mission straight away. Listen. Read the body language of the other player. When you know what the other player wants, don't block anything. Adapt and be flexible. Be *strategically generous.*

Note: These improvisations offer lots of scope for discussion about human behaviour and alternative outcomes amongst the viewers and the players.

STRANGE ENCOUNTERS: Essentially this challenge is similar to *Secret Missions* and *Precious Objects*. It requires the same skills; *imagination, generosity, listening* and *shared discovery*, but it is set in a more surreal, transpersonal, archetypical and timeless zone. It tends to invoke an 'other-worldly' trance-like, *dream-like state of awareness.*

Two players are chosen. They are simply invited to play the role of *strangers.* Nothing else is yet known. Without knowing the context of the situation, they are taken away separately, by some other members of the group, and are both given suggested *new roles* to play and *secret missions.*

When they return, I give a mystical setting in which they are to meet. I do not know what characters they have been given to play, nor what their missions are. We now have three random components in the improvisational equation that can be taken literally anywhere. For example (these are actual scenarios that have manifested):

1. Player A has been told that s/he is a detective exploring a murder case.
2. Player B has been told that s/he is a time traveller, just landed on Earth, trying to understand humans.
3. I have told them that the place is 'a secret garden'.

OR

1. Player A has been told that s/he is a spider-woman-type-goddess waiting for her prey.
2. Player B has been told that s/he is an archaeologist looking for ancient signs.
3. I have told them that the place is 'an underground cave'.

OR

1. Player A has been told: s/he is a little girl who has lost her ball.
2. Player B has been told: s/he is a drunken tramp, sleeping rough.
3. I have told them that the place is 'on the shore of a beautiful lake'.

OR

1. Player A has been told: s/he is a dim-wit, who wants to learn to fly.
2. Player B has been told: s/he is a queen who is locked in a tower.
3. I have told them that the place is 'a bombed building in a major city'.

Note: This type of transpersonal setting awakens the symbolic and mythical, orientating the players gradually towards the later *Archetypical Explorations* (in *Games – Part 4: The Underbelly*).

ANIMAL ENVELOPES: As the name suggests, this game involves being an animal (part animal, part human) while playing within the boundaries of the invisible white lines. Most players love it and get a lot out of it. Others cringe and shy away from it. I can understand this. Those that object to being half animal can either sit and watch or accept the challenge. It opens up discussions about why they struggle with this particular challenge. Either way, it is fascinating to watch, informative on many levels and often excruciatingly funny in a brilliant, cathartic way.

The players are invited to think of their *favourite animal*, which they are asked to keep secret. Two players are then given *secret missions* separately ... *without anyone knowing what animal they have chosen*! I will shortly give examples of the type of missions that work in this context, but first I need to explain what happens, so that it all makes sense.

The two players are asked to stand in opposite corners of the invisible envelope and begin by playing exactly as they did in the *Tension Envelopes* game, exploring the dynamics between them, while only walking on the invisible white lines.

At first the players are clearly human, but gradually they are invited to *immerse* themselves in the breath, feelings and sounds of the animal they have chosen. They should be encouraged to do this without trying to imitate animals in a superficial or clichéd way and without worrying about what they look like! They should enter the 'being' of the animal *via the eyes and the breath ... as if looking through the eyes or Mask of the animal they have secretly chosen*. This requires an intense internal focus, with the result that the players begin to take on very unusual body shapes, half-human and half-animal, while making strange sounds, movements and interesting facial contortions. When they have found their *half-human-half-animal* character, they can begin to focus on the secret mission they have received. For example:

A has chosen to be a Wild Cat and has received the secret mission to 'capture and eat the other animal'.

B has chosen to be an Elephant and has received the secret mission to 'dance with the other animal'.

OR

A has chosen to be an Ant and has received the secret mission to 'attempt to drag the other animal to its nest.'

B has chosen to be a Peacock and has received the secret mission to 'flirt with the other animal'.

OR

A has chosen to be a Wolf and has received the secret mission to 'protect her babies', which are in one of the corners.

B has chosen to be a Penguin and has received the secret mission to 'give the other animal a big hug.'

This game pushes physical and psychic boundaries! The players find themselves exploring extremes of physical and vocal expression that are very daring, but also humorous and liberating. It evokes some extraordinarily bizarre behaviour, which is a wonder to watch. The element of *random absurdity and comedy* is key to making this game more accessible and entertaining for both the viewers and the players. For example, I once witnessed a tall man in his 60's being an ant carrying a leaf on his back. He was a escaping from a small woman who was being an elephant that wanted to make love to him!

Even so, some players find this game a 'bit weird'. It really does stretch anyone's imagination. I'm also aware that there is a stigma attached to imitating or becoming animals. People associate being trees or animal spirits with hippy-dippy, airy-fairy concepts or shamanism, without completely understanding how important these things are. But, to be honest, that never bothers me. Everyone has their fears, beliefs or resistances to something or other. I take risks. I encourage the players to take risks too.

> **One runs risks, but I consider that in the present-day conditions they are worth running.**
>
> Antonin Artaud, 1896-1948, French dramatist, poet, actor and theatre director. *Theatre and it's Double* 1964:59

THE GAMES
Part 4: THE UNDERBELLY

WE ARE NOW entering the section of games that takes the players directly to the HEART and the UNDERBELLY of the process. This is the intimate zone of the 'as yet unspoken', where the invisible, that which we don't want to see or be seen is hidden in the realm of the Shadow. This is where acting becomes dangerous. Danger being one of the seven qualities that outstanding actors have ... alongside *Warmth, Generosity, Enthusiasm, Presence, Grit and Charisma* [Ken Rea – *The Outstanding Actor* – 2015].

In the 'real' world, we are separated from our true potential. In mainstream theatre, one can't even play with real fire anymore, because of health and safety regulations! It's absurd. We must learn to take risks again.

> **We cannot continue to prostitute the idea of theatre whose only value lies in its agonizing magic relationship to reality and danger.**
>
> Antonin Artaud, *The Theatre of Cruelty*

Whether we are afraid or not, the only *way* to go both physically and psychically into the terrain of the dangerous, is to go there with love. Naked. Exposed. No frills attached ... and with no guarantee of security or money back.

We have to go into the unknown, the unspoken and dark side of existence, towards that which attracts us and makes us afraid at the same time. Only in this way can we recognise our true potential. We have to go there together, towards that which we know is our own. That is where the truth is. And yes, we are afraid. We are afraid of being vulnerable. We are afraid of the exposure of hidden parts of ourselves. We are afraid to be confronted with the common Self. But that's what being powerful is all about.

FEELINGS

SENSE MEMORY: I am now going to give an in-depth description of the acting technique, which I have mentioned a few times already in various contexts (see *Chapter 4 – The Mirror/Memory and Imagination; Chapter 5 – Emotional Intelligence/Gitte; Games – Part 3: Transformation/Changing State/Internal Approach*).

As explained earlier, this is a technique that actors can use to reach peak emotions on cue. Its value in the context of confidence building is that it enables the player to access and understand emotions that they would normally suppress or not easily express.

It is definitely a useful resource in the development of emotional intelligence and self-awareness, but it has to be used wisely, in a setting of trust and confidentiality and with the proviso of follow up support, where necessary. I personally would only introduce this acting technique to non-actors in the context of a *course of sessions*, where one has opportunities to revisit the same emotional experience from a range of perspectives and in a variety of creative ways.

So here it is! I give all the players something to write with. I ask them to remember a moment in time when they felt UPSET, ANGRY, STRESSED, FEARFUL ... or (if they don't want to go to dark places) when they felt EXCITED, JOYOUS, IN LOVE. Whatever the emotion they want to explore, whatever instinctively feels right for them is perfect. The intuitive part of our being knows what it wants and where it needs to go. The memory could have come from yesterday, last week or twenty years ago ... from remote childhood even, if they feel they *want* or *need* to explore that.

When they all indicate that they are ready, I tell them that I am going to ask them some questions about the chosen memory, which they can answer in writing in a realistic, abstract or poetical way. I then ask them (this is the dangerous bit) to bring the memory into the NOW, 'as if' it is happening to them RIGHT NOW. When I can see that they are all emotionally engaged with the remembered experience (I can see this in their eyes and body-language), I begin to ask them questions:

> Where are you?
> What time of day is it?
> What's the light like?
> Who is with you?
> What sounds do you hear?
> What are you feeling?
> What is your breathing like?

What's your heart doing?
What are your eyes doing?
What are your hands doing?
What are your feet doing?
How does your skin feel?
What colours do you see around you?
What can you smell?
What do you want?
What are you saying or ... what would you like to say?

I give them plenty of time to reflect, feel and write in between the questions. When they have answered all the questions, they will all have an abstract piece of writing that may look something like this:

I'm in the living room.
Late morning.
Sun streaming in through the windows.
My family.
A lawn mower outside. The budgie chirping in its cage.
Anger.
Short shallow breaths.
My heart is racing.
I feel tears welling.
I'm clenching my fists.
My feet are stuck to the ground.
Hot. Burning around my ears and kneck. My throat hurts.
Magnolia.
Coffee. Dogs.
I want to scream.
I AM NOT INVISIBLE!

I invite the players to read out what they have written in front of the rest of the group, as a type of experiential performance, a *gift* they can share ... but, again, this is their choice. If a player is willing, and most of them are, s/he is invited to stand in the stage area and once again bring the memory into the NOW, imaginatively *seeing, hearing, feeling and sensing every aspect of that moment in time.* When they read what they have written, it is 'as if' it is taking place right there and then. They are totally 'in it' and emotionally connected with the moment. The final phrase tends to be delivered with all the power of their emotions, being possibly the first time that they have dared to put words to what they feel inside openly.

Note: After all the players have presented their abstract texts, we usually have a good shake out and spend some time discussing, reflecting on what just happened, perhaps over a cup of tea. The shared experiences tend to bring out even deeper layers and revelations. After which, we return to playing some really silly games again. (See *Back to Silliness* at the end of this Chapter!)

MONOLOGUES FROM THE HEART: This creative challenge is again designed to provide space for the gift, the sacrifice, the offering of the as yet unspoken.

I give the players paper and pens and ask them to write (at the top and bottom edge of the paper) *the beginning and end sentence of a monologue.* I then invite them to creatively write a short monologue, a rant, a rap, a poem or a soliloquy (text spoken by one person to the audience) that links the beginning and the end sentences somehow. They can write from imagination or they can 'personalize it' i.e. make the content about something they feel deeply on a personal level. They can also do both. Real experiences, feelings and emotions are brilliant sources of inspiration for imaginative works. *There is nothing stranger than reality.*

It is also true that the more rooted the monologues are in authentic feelings, expressions from the heart, the more fascinating and compelling they will be for many. The personal is the universal.

Before they begin writing, I explain to them that they need to write the middle section in a way that they will be able to *memorize it easily.* This is because they will be invited to perform what they have written. The performance doesn't have to be word perfect. An improvised version is fine; something that may simply require remembering two or three bullet points along the way. They could also choose to use the pegging systems of memorisation as explored with the *Surreal Poems* (*Games – Part 2: Imagination*).

When they have grasped what the challenge is and how to proceed, I give them 5-10 mins to write their monologue, as well as prepare the performance of it. Here are some examples of beginning and end sentences, plus a case study of a player's creation:

> 'When I woke up this morning, I knew that something had changed ...
> I knew the world would never be the same again.'

> 'I was trapped ... suddenly I was free.'

> 'I've never told anyone this before ... and that's the truth.'

> 'If there's one thing I can't stand ... It's all in the mind, you see.'

ROBIN, 70 YEARS OLD, ENGLISH: Robin, despite his age, has the versatility, physicality and playful imagination of a child. He stands on his head for long periods of time every day and bathes naked in the ocean at all times of the year. Robin is quite short. In fact, one could say that he is a very small man, not in build, but in height, with a very young, innocent appearance. He has big bright blue eyes, even at 70 yrs old. A sweet person. He shared this with us:

> *'I've never told anyone this before* ... *when I was a young boy, I used to dream of being a jockey, because I was so small. My family was indirectly connected with the world of horse racing, so it wasn't a completely mad dream. One day, I was invited to go to an interview for a job as an apprentice jockey at some racing stables near Aylesbury. I got the placement and I was over the moon!!! But, when I got there I realised that all the other jockeys were midgets. I mean real midgets. That was the first and only time I have ever felt like a giant in my life!! The stable owner ended up advising me to give up the idea of being a jockey, because I was too tall. So, I quit the job. I deeply regret taking his advice to this day, because actually I could have stayed on as a stable hand. The fact is, I love horses* ... *and that's the truth.'*

Note: These monologues can be played in any way the player wants e.g.

- With as much eye contact with the audience as possible

- As a monologue to a player of choice in the stage area, whose task is to silently, but supportively listen

- In the round, with the rest of the group seated in a circle around the player

- As a monologue to oneself, as if one is totally alone in an isolated bubble of consciousness ... or looking in the mirror.

As the players become more inventive, they tend to create all sorts of new 'theatrical' options. They begin to self-direct. One player performed his creation, while precariously balancing on a whole stack of chairs. Another crouched in a corner with her back to us. Others reach out for audience participation. One wanted to lie on the floor on her back and have the rest of the group moving around her, looking down on her from above. Another shouted the monologue through the wall from the next room, demanding to know if we were listening.

All variations, have the potential to reveal the human heart and spirit in intimate and surprising ways.

Very Advanced Note: With this particular challenge I find opportunities to draw the players' attention to a conscious use EYES in relationship with the target or audience ... the eyes being the doors of the soul and the windows of the heart. EYES have a whole language of their own. This is a theme that deserves a whole chapter, but can only ineffectively be described in a book. The same is true for the explanation of what an isolated *bubble of consciousness* is, which in theatrical terms is sometimes called the 1st circle of awareness. Both have to be experienced and witnessed to be understood.

ONE MINUTE RITUAL: This is another creative challenge that provides a way of exploring the 'as yet unspoken' and making the invisible visible. It evolved out of an idea I got from reading about Strasberg's method of training actors.

Lee Strasberg (1901-1982) was an American actor, director and very well-known acting teacher. He was the founder of the famous Actor's Studio in New York. As part of the training, Strasberg occasionally asked his students to prepare and present a short performance of something that they *had never revealed to anyone before in their life*. One actress chose to dance for the first time in front of a group of people, being something she normally did alone in her room.

The impact of such a sensitive revelation is like a sacrificial gift to the audience. It is spontaneous, living theatre of a very special kind.

After a constellation of players have been with me for at least 5-6 sessions, when they have bonded and I have gained their trust, I invite them all to think about something that they *have never or very rarely told or shown anyone in their life before* ... something that they feel might be important for the rest of the group to know.

I suggest that they go home and sleep on the idea for a week or two. When they have an idea, they should prepare a little visual performance piece that helps us understand what this means to them. I give a few examples of how it could be abstractly and artistically presented in the form of:

> *a poem they have written*
> *a piece of writing they have never shown or read to anyone before*
> *an excerpt from a book they consider to have great significance*
> *a song they want to sing*
> *a dance or a series of movements to music*
> *a martial arts demonstration ... or other skill*
> *a painting ... they can even paint a picture on stage*
> *the telling of a story or the relating of a dream*
> *a symbolic ritual of sorts*

I invite them to use candles, lighting, music, costume, mask, props, objects, puppets, drapes, signs and symbols, photos, videos, projections ... anything they want. I tell them it need only last *one minute* (or even less), but that it could also last five or ten minutes. They can use their creative instincts to decide what would capture and hold an audience's attention.

I also give them a couple of examples of *One Minute Rituals* that have been created by other players in the past:

HELEN, 24 YEARS OLD, BRITISH: was a highly sensitive and introverted player. Helen had problems closing her eyes and lifting her arms higher than her heart in trust games. It seemed she was protecting her body from something. Helen's *One Minute Ritual* was as follows:

She arrived on stage covered in layers of clothing. She knelt on the ground and placed a large bowl and a box of matches in front of her. Slowly she began to remove the outer layers of her clothing, layer by layer. On each layer were stuck bits of torn paper with words like ... *Self-Hate, Loathing, Stupid, Pain, Guilt, Revenge, Stink, Filth, Waste, Fear, Silence, Disgust, Dirty, Confusion, Anger, Loneliness.* As she removed the layers, she ripped the bits of paper off the clothes and placed them in the bowl in front of her and set light to them. Yes, real fire.

MATHEW, 26 YEARS OLD, BRITISH: When I first met him in the Playground, Mathew was strangely and quirkily creative, but rather insecure and still living at home with Mum, Dad and his younger brother. He had, from the outset, a wonderful imagination, but also a very slight speech defect. He appeared to have an unusual form of naivety about the 'real world'. Mathew's *One Minute Ritual* was as follows:

He placed a small low round table in the centre of the stage. He also set up a cassette recorder with a tape he turned on to play. He then sat crouched on the table with his back to us and placed his hands over his ears. For about fifteen seconds we did not hear anything and there was no movement. We waited in suspense. Gradually the sound became audible. It was a chaotic and harsh sound ... noise really, that got louder and louder. As the sound increased, Mathew started banging his ears and became more and more agitated and distressed. Slowly he turned to face the audience and looked terrified, covering his ears. In the discussion afterwards, Mathew revealed to us that for the first seven years of his life he had been deaf, until suddenly the outside world's sounds had invaded his inner reality ... his inner sanctum.

Mathew continued to come to my sessions for several years. He clearly felt very safe in Playground and began to blossom as an exceptionally talented visual artist. He is now creating complex, futuristic comic books, painting surreal art works and presenting visual public performances about his struggles with the outer world, which in the past were periodically secretly expressed through self-harm.

GRAHAM, 35 YEARS OLD, BRITISH: When Graham joined the Playground, he had already worked in theatre for many years as a professional stage manager, having trained at Bristol Old Vic Theatre School in Stage Management. When I first encountered him, I found it quite hard to understand what he was saying or to hold any form of eye contact with him, and yet it was clear that he was highly intelligent and experienced in professional theatre. He had also studied clowning and magic tricks. His *One Minute Ritual* was as follows:

Graham didn't say anything throughout the whole ritual (which lasted 2-3 minutes). Not until the very end. He took several large pieces of white paper, sellotaped them together and laid the whole piece out on the floor. Then with a large, black, permanent marker pen he drew what looked like the lines of a brick wall all over it. He then held it up in front of himself, for us all to see. It was indeed a wall. He said: 'That's me.'

In the discussion afterwards, Graham told us that he had been severely bullied at school. He found it very difficult to make any real friends and almost impossible to talk to people, no matter whether they were men or women. After a couple of years of playing in the Playground, this is what he wrote as feedback:

> '[I have gained] the confidence to interact on a personal level that is devoid of any pre-supposed notions. In life meeting people and interacting with them has a purpose. This could be for work, networking, sport, hobbies, etc. In improvisation there is no fixed agenda, and whereas I would normally find it difficult to meet and converse with a relative stranger with no specific reason for that meeting, with improvisation I can interact freely, without fear of rejection, with either gender and with confidence. [The most important aspect of the playground is] becoming someone else, in a controlled and safe environment, utilising characteristics and emotions that I can feel but also control, with people that I can trust and have empathy for. [What I have enjoyed most is] being able to push emotional boundaries knowing that it is only playacting; also seeing other people as well as myself learning and experiencing changes in their ability to let go.'

Graham now has an MA degree in Arts Administration and teaches this subject on a professional level. He has also founded his own theatre company. He can now hold direct eye contact with 'normal' people and is very outspoken and passionate about the importance of creative teaching.

DOING NOTHING

''If it's not easy, darling, you are not doing it right!' was repeatedly said by Rudi Shelley (one of the tutors at B.O.V.T.S.). But what's easy?! Getting to the place of understanding what easy means is not easy, but when you get there experientially it becomes clear.

In the acting business (particularly in film) we say: 'Less is more.' The same is true of life. *If you do less, you achieve more. The simplest solution is usually the right one.* This is one of the hardest things for the players in the Playground to grasp. And yet, as I mentioned earlier, 'DO LESS', 'SLOW DOWN', 'BE STILL', 'KEEP IT SIMPLE' are probably the most important pieces of advice I can give anyone. In life and in theatre. In the theatre of life.

There is enormous power in stillness.

When you do nothing, you come closer to your Self. You give yourself the time to sense and feel, and in that space you will intuitively find what it is you are looking for ... or even something you may not be looking for! *It will come to you*. In that sense, doing nothing means you are already doing all you need to do, which is *breath* and *feel*. You are not forcing things to happen.

Of course there will always be moments of wildness and chaos. We are like water and the weather. We are all a part of nature. But in terms of acting and conscious choice, *being still and centred* is one of the most powerful techniques you can employ.

The following games and creative challenges are designed to develop the players understanding of what this means.

THE 'BEING BORING' GAME: I ask all the players to think of a way of performing on stage that is utterly boring to watch. This is very hard to do. It's another one of those paradoxes. When we *try* to be boring or bored, then very often we aren't.

There are inventive ways to be very boring indeed, which I have witnessed. Scratching your car keys over a radiator for three minutes is excruciatingly boring to watch and listen to. Being boring *consciously*, requires a knowledge of what it is NOT to be boring. The things the players come up with are very amusing. A bit of light relief. A great discussion arises out of this game. There's not much more I can say about it. Try it.

THE 'DOING NOTHING' GAME: Three players stand or sit or lie on stage. They do nothing. The audience is held by the silence and the suspense of what might potentially happen.

The players are encouraged, in the nothingness, to go deeply, intuitively *inside*, breathing, feeling and, with the use of peripheral vision to sense each other and the space between them. They are invited to do as little as possible. No-one should feel they have to do anything, unless they really feel the urge. If and when one of the players finally does something, then the other players can react to it in an authentic way, if they feel like it. If it feels right. They can say something if they want. Or not. There are no rules (apart from 'less is more').

Paradoxically, something always happens, even if it is very little. Something comes from nowhere. Whatever happens is fascinating to watch. A twitch, a breath, an inadvertent sigh or a look is captivating. The viewers are engaged, riveted, mesmerised ... using their imagination to interpret what might actually be going on in the players' minds. We want to understand. Strangely enough, it is precisely when the players do nothing that the viewers' fill the empty spaces with their own imaginings.

Note: Being able to do nothing is an essential *life skill*. Knowing when to pause, say nothing ... and then pause a little longer. The real magic being the knowledge of when and how to apply it. As we grow in confidence and self-belief this becomes clearer. It also becomes clearer that the interpretation of what we do is at least 50% in the mind of the observer. This is alchemy's gold, in terms of Self-awareness.

THE NEVER ENDING STORY: The most important qualities of this game are *breath, sound, listening, feeling, emotion, relating through movement, touch, dance, rhythm, stillness and silence, imagination, mirroring* and ... of course, *doing nothing*. In this game the players can use words, one or two words at a time maybe, or some kind of fantasy language, or simply sounds, sighs and utterances.

Two players start, as in *The Doing Nothing Game*, standing, lying or sitting. Out of doing nothing arises a million and one imaginative things. This time the players are invited to follow their gut instincts and expand on authentic feelings that come up, using all their senses and their relationship with the space around them.

Out of this, a whole abstract story or drama begins to emerge.

When a story reaches a peak, a climax or a natural closure ... I send a third player in. Things shift and change. Another relationship. Another constellation. Another dynamic. Another story. After the new dynamics are established, I might ask one of the first two players to leave ... now there are only two on stage again. A new relationship. Things shift and change again. New dynamics occur ... a new part of the story ... and then I send in another player. Again, there are three, and so on and so forth, until all the players in the group have played their part in the unfolding drama. Those that are not on stage watch.

Once, an imaginary fire was spontaneously created centre stage. It never went out. All the players, in turn, tended to it and related to it in different ways. They danced round it, created magic spells with it, cooked with it, explored fire jumping, burnt themselves on it and warmed themselves by it. At one point it exploded and took on a life of its own. It was utterly mesmerising to watch and yet it was invisible.

Anything can happen, from nothing to a riotous free-for-all, always returning to moments of intense symbolic and archetypical stillness and beauty. Imaginary objects, beings, visions, gestures and sounds come up out of nowhere.

THE SHADOW

We recognise symbols and archetypes from ancient stories, myths and our dreams. We identify with some archetypes more than others. They feel familiar. We feel attracted to them. It feels empowering or comforting somehow to associate oneself with them: *the Mother, the Goddess, the Witch, the Teacher, the Healer, the Hero, the Shaman, the Priest, the Clown, the Joker, the Child, the Demon, the Serpent, the Bastard, the Warrior, the Destroyer*. All of these, and many more, appear in differing forms and guises in each of us. We are transformative beings.

If one chose to, one could associate oneself *with two opposing archetypes* that interchange, depending on the circumstances and who we are with, for example: *the Creator and the Destroyer, the Goddess and the Serpent, the Trickster and the Healer*. For certain, there is a dark and a light side in everyone. One could describe these opposites in more earthly forms, for example: the Giver and the Taker, the Brave and the Fearful, the Lustful and the Lonely, the Wild One and the Controller, the Victim and the Oppressor, the Creator and the Saboteur. Both extremes can exist, invariably do exist, in the same person.

This next creative challenge draws upon the inner imagination that is capable of discovering the essential or innate possibilities of opposites within oneself. The information that comes out of it can sometimes be strangely ambiguous to the viewer, but seems to have profound meaning for the player that created it. It represents another invisible layer of unconsciousness self-awareness that becomes conscious.

It goes without saying, I hope, that after all the games we have played so far, each player will by now have a much clearer idea of the paradoxical nature of their own unique *creative being*.

INNATE OPPOSITES: I invite the players to consider the extreme opposites within themselves. Strengths and weaknesses, if you like. Their brilliance ... but also, the part that tries to sabotage their brilliance, perhaps. The light and the dark. Each player knows intuitively what I mean.

Having given them all something to write with, I tell them that I will ask a series of questions, first about *the dark* side of their being and then, the same set of questions, about the light side. I encourage the players to answer the questions in an imaginative, poetical or abstract way (similar to *Sense Memory*), using their intuitive feelings and inner sense of truth. The questions are as follows:

> Who are you?
> What is your name?
> Where do you come from?
> How old are you?
> What are you doing here?
> What do you want?
> Where are you going?
> What causes you pain?
> What do you love?
> Which element do you connect with?
> What colour(s) are you?
> What shape are you?
> What do you desire?
> Why do you desire that?
> What would you like to say to the world?

Afterwards, I invite the players to read what they have written ... if they want to. First the *dark* piece and then the *light*. By now, the players are in tune with this sort of creative challenge and the majority are openly expressive when they read what they have written. Some step into a type of character performance or role-play in order to embody what they have written.

I choose not to comment or say more at this point. A confidential discussion about the various revelations may ensue. But, more often than not, one is simply left with a feeling of wonder and deep intimate silence that can be left as it is. I simply remind the players to watch their dreams. (See *Chapter 4 – The Mirror/The Shadow*).

RETURN TO SILLINESS

At the end of a session, in particular one that has taken the players to deeper, more serious reflections about the *transpersonal nature of being*, it might be a good idea to lead the players' awareness back into the room, into 'real' time and space, the comic and the NOW. The players need to go home feeling earthed, clear headed and aware of the absurd extremes of life. So, to close the four games sections, I am adding a couple of games that are utterly ridiculous, but a great way to round off a play session in a fun way.

JOKE IMITATION: This game is actually a drama exercise that I was made to play over and over again in my second year of drama school at Bristol Old Vic. I suppose, for this reason, I never forgot it. The aim was to get us to think about the art of comedy, but, as a game, it can also be used on an ad hoc basis for pure Bacchanalian fun.

I ask the players if anyone has a joke they can tell, which is not too long and not too short. If no-one can think of a joke, which is often the case when put on the spot, I usually have a couple up my sleeve e.g.

> *A man wakes up in the morning and finds silver slug tracks all over his bed covers. He looks around the room and sees them all over the carpet, down the stairs and all over the living room furniture too. He follows the tracks into the kitchen and finally spots a great big fat slimy slug happily chomping away at some leftover food on a plate. The man is absolutely furious. He picks the slug up, opens the front door and chucks it out, as far away as he can, over the garden hedge into the fields beyond. A month later there's a knock on the front door. The man opens the door. He looks around and can't see anyone. Then he looks down and see's the slug again, looking up at him. The slug says, really sweetly, in a tiny high pitched voice: "What was all that about, then?"*

I tell the joke with gestures, dramatic pauses and a silly voice at the end, so there is plenty of action. I will have warned all the other players to watch the person telling the joke (in this case me) *very carefully*, as I will randomly pick one of the audience members to go on stage afterwards and imitate the way the joker told the joke! The whole group will then have to watch the next joker *very carefully again*, as I will spontaneously pick a third player to imitate the second version of the joke, and so on and so forth ... until the whole group has had a go at imitating the imitation of the imitation. The joke rapidly becomes almost unrecognisable with the inevitable mistakes, loss of memory, switches of voices, laughing and goofiness exaggerated to an extreme and imitated over and over again. It gets worse and worse. Then finally the original joke teller has to go up and imitate the final joker. It's hysterically funny, especially when the players get the hang of exaggerated cartoon-like imitations.

Note: Obviously, it's good for *observational skills and memory*. But the aim is certainly not perfection!

EMOTIONAL PARTY: This game usually turns into the ultimate child-like romp. I have no idea where I got the initial idea from (probably from one of my students a long time ago). It is definitely one of those games that is repeatedly requested by the players.

Let us say, for the purposes of describing the game, that the group has the magical number of nine players. Out of the nine players, I select one player who will be the 'host' of the party. The other eight players are the 'guests' that arrive at the party. I give each player an EMOTION (or type of behaviour) and a NUMBER (in order of the guest's arrival). For example:

Host: ECSTATIC JOY
Guest 1: FURIOUS ANGER
Guest 2: PARANOID FEAR
Guest 3: WRETCHED GRIEF
Guest 4: RAUNCHY DRUNKENESS
Guest 5: LUNATIC MADNESS
Guest 6: DIVAESQUE BITCHYNESS
Guest 7: UTTER CONFUSION
Guest 8: MYSTERIOUS WONDER

I then tell each player to find an inner motivation or convincing reason for being possessed by that emotion and to be prepared to play it to an extreme! I explain that the host will start alone on stage, setting up the party with chairs, cushions and invisible food and drink, while dancing to imaginary music. S/he will be 'ecstatically joyous' about it all. There is a loud vocalised DING DONG!!! ... and the 1st guest arrives in a 'furious rage' (e.g. someone has just smashed into his/her car). The host greets the 1st guest with 'ecstatic joy', but gradually becomes infected by the 1st guest's emotion. Soon they are both 'furiously angry' (e.g. fighting or arguing about why there are no peanuts). Then there is another loudly vocalised DING DONG!!! The 2nd guest arrives in an 'extremely paranoid state' (e.g. the police or the mafia are after him/her). The host and the 1st guest greet the 2nd guest in a 'furious rage', but gradually get infected by the 2nd guest's 'paranoia'. Soon all three players are completely paranoid about everything each other says and does, perhaps hiding behind curtains and chairs, terrified etc. And then the 3rd guest arrives ... and so on and so forth, with all the players getting infected by each new emotion that arrives through the door. The game carries on in the same way until the last guest arrives, where everyone becomes 'mysteriously wonderous'. BUT then ... the last guest leaves! And the whole thing plays BACKWARDS again! They have to go through all the emotions again, in reverse order from 8-1, until the host is left alone on stage, where s/he returns to be 'ecstatically joyous' about the wonderful party!

Note: It's important that the players say: 'DING DONG!!!' really loudly, in order to announce their arrival, or no-one will hear them. This game gets much louder than a children's birthday party! It's also important that when they leave the party, each guest must make their exit dramatically clear or no-one will know when to switch to the next emotion in reverse order. Needless to say, the return journey through the emotions is even more extreme, because they are covering familiar territory. This is exhausting, especially for the host, so, what I tend to do is make sure that the next time we play this game the host is guest No. 8!

So, that was it. This final game is a joy to watch and take part in. The players are stretched and pushed by each other into the boundlessness of their 'being'. Political correctness flies out the window. Players, who initially insisted *they never get angry*, find themselves being inspiringly angry about all sorts of silly things. People who said they were *afraid of being called insane* discover that they can be ingeniously mad and inventive. Intellectuals and academics dance wildly and lose complete control. People who are normally afraid or reserved become cartoon characters of themselves and end up hysterically laughing at everything. Once, in 'lunatic madness', I witnessed a player with his trousers down by his ankles, joyously hopping around saying: 'I am a sardine in a tin!' He happened to be a good friend of his Holiness himself, the Dalai Lama.

So great is the power of joy over men.
I CHING 58 Tui

'A medicine man should not be a saint. He should experience all the ups and downs, the despair and joy, the magic and the reality, the courage and the fear, of his people. He should be able to sink as low as a bug, or soar as high as an eagle. Unless he can experience both, he is no good as a medicine man. Sickness, jail, poverty, getting drunk. I had to experience all that myself. Sinning makes the world go around. You can't be so stuck up inuuman that you want to be pure, your soul wrapped up in a plastic bag all the time. You have to be god and the devil, both of them. Being a good medicine man means being right in the midst of the turmoil, not shielding yourself from it. It means experiencing life in all its phases. It means not being afraid of cutting up and playing the fool now and then. That's sacred too. Nature, the Great Spirit, they are not perfect. The world couldn't stand that perfection. The spirit has a good side and a bad side. Sometimes the bad side gives more knowledge than the good.'

– Lame Deer

AFTERWORD

WHAT NEXT?

There is more in a human life than our theories of it allow. Sooner or later something seems to call us onto a particular path. You may remember this "something" as a signal moment in childhood when an urge out of nowhere, a fascination, a peculiar turn of events struck like an annunciation: This is what I must do, this is what I've got to have. This is who I am.

James Hillman, *The Soul's Code* 1997:3

WHEN THE PLAYERS leave the Playground, I don't have to advise them about what to do next. They know. They have developed a new consciousness. Conscience. Whatever. They know they can do pretty much anything they *want* to do. They have a choice. They are now their own creative observer. They can now create their own Playground or simply be that which they were born to be; a pioneer in their particular 'gift'. They know that they are essentially a unique being that has a lot to give. In doing that, they have the possibility of changing the world they live in.

Just one last story, before I close. The other day, I asked my group of players (who had been playing with me for six months or more) to close their eyes and imagine two portraits of their SELF. I suggested that the first should be a portrait of their suppressed, down trodden SELF ... the part of them that felt small and weak. They all looked confused and said: 'What?', 'What are you talking about?', 'I don't understand', 'Can you repeat that, please?', 'What are we supposed to do?', 'Eeer, isn't it time for a tea break?' They genuinely didn't understand or didn't want to understand what I meant. They literally 'blanked out' on me.

So, I said: 'O.K. Forget it. We'll move onto the second portrait.' I invited them to see a portrait of their inner creative being, joyous, happy, confident and free. Without another word, they all immediately closed their eyes and began to smile, imagine and dream. The frowns disappeared from the faces. They looked completely blissed out.

The *inner voice* knows where we need to go. All we have to do is listen to it. Our intuitive intelligence looks after us. Even when we are asleep. Don't let anyone silence it. And just keep *playing* and *acting* with all your heart, guts and strength ... 'as if' your life depended on it.

With that I can confirm that there has not been one session, in the forty odd years of developing these oases for child-like play, that has not brought me to the point of tears ... no, not just the point, but over the edge, tears streaming down my face, either from side-splitting laughter or from some deep emotional connection. My glass runneth over.

Josephine Larsen – May 2016

Some Books That Have Influenced The Way I See Things Now
(*in order of 1st publication*)

Alice in Wonderland – Lewis Carol 1865

The Theatre and It's Double – Antonin Artaud 1938

In Search of the Miraculous – P. D. Ouspenski 1949

On the Technique of Acting – Michael Chekhov 1953

Motivation and Personality – Abraham H. Maslow 1954

Memories, Dreams and Reflections – C. G. Jung 1963

The Teaching of Don Juan: A Yaqui Way of Knowledge – Carlos Castaneda 1968

The Empty Space – Peter Brook 1968

Impro – Keith Johnstone – Methuen 1981

Improvisation in Drama – Anthony Frost & Ralph Yarrow – Macmillan 1990

Meeting The Shadow: The Hidden Power of the Dark Side of Human Nature – Edited by Connie Zweig and Jeremiah Abrams 1991

Games for Actors and Non-Actors – Augusto Boal 1992

The Spell of the Sensuous – David Abram 1996

The Soul's Code – James Hillman 1996

The Cosmic Serpent – Jeremy Narby 1998

The Field – Lynne McTaggart 2001

The Psychopath Test – Jon Ronson 2011

Vortex of Energy – David Ash 2012

The Outstanding Actor – Ken Rea 2015

ABOUT THE AUTHOR

JOSEPHINE LARSEN'S professional career can be tracked through the Berlin Cabaret scene, French Cult Film, German Rock Opera, Experimental Fringe, State Funded Classical Theatre, Poetry in Performance, as well as German, American and British T.V., FILM and RADIO. In parallel, and unknown to many, Josephine has been working constantly as an innovative teacher, inspiring new waves of creative thought with the development of her unique system for coaching actors and non-actors in the power of imagination, intuitive confidence and creative SELF-expression.

In 1995 family circumstances led her to return to the UK, where she continued to work professionally, training additionally in psychology, teaching and researching into the untapped imaginative genius of the human mind. Although she returns often to Berlin, Josephine is currently based in Devon, England. She is a mother of two and a grandmother of two, a maverick, alchemist and revolutionary spirit, who is devoted to individual empowerment and freedom from oppression.

www.josephinelarsen.com

ARTIST AND DESIGNER LOUISE BURSTON lives and works in the seaside town of Burry Port, situated on the Carmarthenshire coastline. Louise has exhibited widely and has work in public and private collections. She has a BA and MA in Fine Art and is a contextual studies lecturer at Swansea College of Art and Design. In 2009 Louise set up the Zero Lubin brand, together with writer Gerry King. The company publishes and promotes short stories, colouring books, greetings cards and prints and collaborates with other artists and writers.

louiseburston.wordpress.com

NOTES

NOTES